THE CAMBRIDGE EDITION OF THE WORKS OF F. SCOTT FITZGERALD

For Charles T. Scott

Gatsby was never quite real to me. His original served for a good enough exterior until about the middle of the book he grew thin and I began to fill him with my own emotional life. So he's synthetic — and that's one of the flaws in this book

F. Scott Fitzgerald
Ellerslie
Edgemoor
Delaware
1927

Fitzgerald's inscription to Charles T. Scott in a first edition of *The Great Gatsby*. Special Collections, Michigan State University Libraries.

TRIMALCHIO

An Early Version of *The Great Gatsby*

* * *

F. SCOTT FITZGERALD

Edited by
JAMES L. W. WEST III

CAMBRIDGE
UNIVERSITY PRESS

CAMBRIDGE UNIVERSITY PRESS

Cambridge, New York, Melbourne, Madrid, Cape Town, Singapore,
São Paulo, Delhi, Dubai, Tokyo, Mexico City

Cambridge University Press
The Edinburgh Building, Cambridge CB2 8RU, UK

Published in the United States of America by Cambridge University Press, New York

www.cambridge.org
Information on this title: www.cambridge.org/9780521890472

First published 2000
Reprinted 2000
First paperback edition 2002

A catalogue record for this publication is available from the British Library

ISBN 978-0-521-40237-8 Hardback
ISBN 978-0-521-89047-2 Paperback

CONTENTS

ACKNOWLEDGMENTS

For the opportunity to publish this edition of *Trimalchio* I thank Eleanor Lanahan, Thomas P. Roche, Jr., and the late Samuel J. Lanahan, Trustees of the F. Scott Fitzgerald Estate. My thanks go also to Chris Byrne of Harold Ober Associates, Inc., and to Andrew Brown of Cambridge University Press.

The work of this edition was made possible by a fellowship from the National Endowment for the Humanities and a travel grant from the American Philosophical Society; for this support I am most grateful.

Princeton University Library continues to help advance the Cambridge Fitzgerald Edition in numerous ways. I thank William L. Joyce, Don Skemer, Stephen Ferguson, Margaret M. Sherry, AnnaLee Pauls, Charles E. Greene, and Jane Snedeker for their assistance. Patrick Scott and Paul Schultz at the Thomas Cooper Library, University of South Carolina, have provided courteous and essential aid.

The Pennsylvania State University has given generous support. My thanks to Susan Welch and Ray Lombra of the College of the Liberal Arts and to Don Bialostosky of the Department of English. Special thanks to Robert R. Edwards, Randy J. Ploog, Susan Reighard, Carol Ann Mindrup, Suzanne Simmons, and Pannay Burt of the Institute for the Arts and Humanistic Studies. I am grateful to Kathryn M. Plank for sharing with me her insights about *Trimalchio*. LaVerne Kennevan Maginnis has given much assistance with textual labors; Christopher Weinmann (Magister Evidentis) has worked tirelessly on annotations and collations. John Hruschka gave last-minute assistance. I thank them all.

Permission to publish Illustrations 1, 2, and 3, and the image on the rear panel of the dust jacket, has been granted by the Manuscripts Division, Department of Rare Books and Special Collections, Princeton University Libraries. The inscription reproduced as the frontispiece is published with the permission of Special Collections, Michigan State University Libraries. (I am grateful to Robert A. Martin for bringing this inscribed copy to my attention.) The photograph of Tommy Hitchcock (Illustration 4) appears courtesy of the Museum of Polo and Hall of Fame; the picture of Edith Cummings (Illustration 5) is reproduced by permission of the United States Golf Association.

J.L.W.W. III

ILLUSTRATIONS
(Beginning on page 179)

Frontispiece. Fitzgerald's inscription to Charles T. Scott in a first edition of *The Great Gatsby*

CHRONOLOGY OF COMPOSITION AND PUBLICATION

JUNE 1922 Fitzgerald conceives ideas and themes for a third novel while correcting proofs for *Tales of the Jazz Age* at White Bear Lake, Minnesota.

SUMMER 1923 He produces 18,000 words; most of this material is later discarded, but he salvages the short story "Absolution," published in June 1924.

APRIL 1924 Fitzgerald reconceives the novel; he tells Maxwell Perkins, his editor at Scribners, that it will be a "consciously artistic achievement."

SUMMER 1924 Fitzgerald completes the first draft of the novel in France and begins revising the text.

OCTOBER 1924 He finishes the novel and mails it to Scribners on 27 October; its title is "The Great Gatsby."

NOVEMBER 1924 Perkins sends criticisms to Fitzgerald in letters dated 18 and 20 November. Fitzgerald changes the title to "Trimalchio in West Egg."

DECEMBER 1924 Two sets of galley proofs are mailed to Fitzgerald at the end of the month; he reverts to "The Great Gatsby" as his title.

JANUARY–FEBRUARY 1925 Fitzgerald revises galleys in Rome and Capri; he returns master proofs to Perkins and continues to suggest other titles, including "Trimalchio."

MARCH 1925 Resetting, corrections, and checking at Scribners. The title is fixed as "The Great Gatsby."

10 APRIL 1925 Publication of the first edition.

INTRODUCTION

". . . I've shifted things around a good deal to make people wonder."
– Jay Gatsby to Nick Carraway, *Trimalchio*, Chapter VIII

Reading F. Scott Fitzgerald's *Trimalchio*, an early and complete version of *The Great Gatsby*, is like listening to a well-known musical composition, but played in a different key and with an alternate bridge passage. A theme that one usually hears in the middle movement is now heard in the last. Familiar leitmotifs play through the work but appear at unexpected moments. Several favorite passages are missing, but new combinations and sequences, recognizably from the hand of the composer, are present. To the knowledgeable listener it is like hearing the same work and yet a different work.

I. HISTORY OF THE TEXT

Fitzgerald began to think seriously about the novel that would become *Trimalchio*, and later *The Great Gatsby*, in June 1922. He was living at White Bear Lake in Minnesota, near his home town of St. Paul; he was working on the proofs for *Tales of the Jazz Age*, his second collection of short stories. Fitzgerald labored for short stretches on this new novel during the next two years but was dissatisfied with what he wrote. The material he was working with was different from what he eventually decided to use for *Gatsby*. The locale of this novel, he said, was "the middle west and New York of 1885," and the story had "a catholic element."[1] Fitzgerald

---

[1] Fitzgerald to Maxwell Perkins, *c.* 20 June 1922. The letters between Fitzgerald and Perkins that surround the composition and publication of the novel have been published in *Dear Scott/Dear Max: The Fitzgerald–Perkins Correspondence*, ed.

never completed a full text of this narrative; only two holograph leaves survive from the drafts that he did produce.[2] From these early efforts he salvaged the short story "Absolution," published in the *American Mercury* for June 1924 and collected in *All the Sad Young Men.*

By early April 1924 Fitzgerald had reconceived his novel. In a well-known letter, written from Great Neck, Long Island (where he and his wife Zelda were living), he told Maxwell Perkins, his editor at Charles Scribner's Sons, that his new narrative would be "purely creative work" and that it would draw on "the sustained imagination of a sincere and yet radiant world."[3] Fitzgerald began setting down this novel, in holograph, sometime that spring. He continued to compose through the summer of 1924 while living in Saint-Raphaël on the French Riviera; by September he had completed an initial draft. He spent the early fall putting his narrative through a succession of revised typescripts and promised to send the novel to Perkins in October. He made good on that vow: on 27 October he placed a final typescript in the transatlantic mail.

On that day Fitzgerald ceased his labors and formally moved his novel into the public phase of its existence. He submitted it to the "publication process," a loose term for a sequence of mechanical and commercial operations which would, as he knew, transform it from a literary artifact in one copy to a saleable commodity in multiple copies. Naturally he expected to see proofs, and surely he planned to do some revising on them, but there is no evidence that, on 27 October, he contemplated major rewriting or structural revisions. He had completed this version of his novel.

As it turned out, however, Fitzgerald did make major changes in

---

John Kuehl and Jackson R. Bryer (New York: Scribners, 1971): 60–94; this letter appears on pp. 60–1.

[2] See Matthew J. Bruccoli, "'An Instance of Apparent Plagiarism': F. Scott Fitzgerald, Willa Cather, and the First *Gatsby* Manuscript," *Princeton University Library Chronicle* 39 (Spring 1978): 171–8. Images of the two manuscript leaves are reproduced in the article.

[3] Fitzgerald to Perkins, *c.* 10 April 1924, *Dear Scott/Dear Max*, p. 70. For an account of the composition, revision, and subsequent textual history of the novel, see the introduction to the Cambridge edition of *The Great Gatsby* (1991), ed. Matthew J. Bruccoli, pp. ix–xli.

the galleys. He decided to do so partly on his own but was influenced also by Perkins' reactions to the typescript. These criticisms came to him in letters dated 18 and 20 November.[4] Perkins was generous with his praise: "The novel is a wonder," he wrote in the first letter, adding in the second that Fitzgerald had produced "an extraordinary book." Perkins complimented Fitzgerald's narrative approach and was much taken by the irony and symbolism of the novel. "It's magnificent!" he wrote.

Perkins also had suggestions, however, nearly all of them centering on Jay Gatsby. The character was "somewhat vague," he complained: "The reader's eyes can never quite focus upon him." Perkins asked for more physical details about Gatsby, so that he might be seen "as vividly as Daisy and Tom are, for instance." Perkins also wanted an explanation, or at least several hints, about the sources of Gatsby's money. Most importantly, he suggested to Fitzgerald that the story of Gatsby's past not be withheld until nearly the end of the novel – as it was in the typescript. Perhaps Gatsby's career could "come out bit by bit in the course of actual narrative."

After mailing these remarks to Fitzgerald, Perkins sent the typescript to the Scribner Press for typesetting. Such a course of action seems curious to us today. If Perkins was suggesting changes, why did he not let Fitzgerald produce a revised typescript and then send that text to the compositors as setting copy? The explanations for Perkins' behavior are several. First, he probably did not anticipate major and thoroughgoing revisions. Fitzgerald had done little revising in the proofs of his previous five books with Scribners; probably he would only shift some material about and do some stylistic tinkering. Second, Fitzgerald was in Europe and communication with him was slow. If the novel was to be ready for the spring publishing season, it needed to be moved into production immediately. Perkins began the process by having the text typeset.

Third and most important, Charles Scribner's Sons owned and operated its own printing plant. The Scribner Press was located at

---

[4] These two letters are reproduced in full in Appendix 1 of this edition. In *Dear Scott/Dear Max*, the date of the 18 November letter is given as 14 November (p. 82).

311 West 43rd Street in New York City; all printing and binding for the parent firm was executed there. The editors who worked in the Scribner Building at 597 Fifth Avenue had close and immediate control over printing operations at the Scribner Press and could usually count on efficient turnaround of proofs.[5] What is more, the costs of letterpress composition during this period of U.S. book publishing were not as large (relative to the entire expense of producing a book) as they would later become. In the late 1920s and early 1930s, for example, Perkins customarily had the novels of Thomas Wolfe typeset before he and Wolfe got down to serious editorial work on them. Perkins followed this same pattern with Ernest Hemingway's *A Farewell to Arms* (1929), *Death in the Afternoon* (1932), and *To Have and Have Not* (1937), all produced while Hemingway was living outside the United States.[6] Thus Perkins' decision to put Fitzgerald's novel immediately into galleys appears not to have been unusual for him – not greatly different from having a stenographer make a clean typescript.

The composition was done in late December, and galley proofs went to Fitzgerald in two batches. Double sets of each batch were mailed, a working set for Fitzgerald to keep and a master set to be marked and returned to Perkins. The first batch of proofs was sent to the author on 27 December, the second batch on the 30th. Fitzgerald undertook a complicated rewriting and restructuring of the novel in these proofs, once they reached him in January. He followed his own instincts for revision but also paid attention to Perkins' advice. On his own, he rewrote Chapters VI and VII; reacting to Perkins' suggestions, he moved much material concerning Jay Gatsby's past to earlier positions in the novel and added short paragraphs to account for Gatsby's wealth. He polished the prose extensively and introduced several new

---

[5] For information about the Scribner Press during this period, see *The House of Scribner, 1905–1930*, ed. John Delaney (Detroit: Gale Research Inc., 1997).

[6] See Francis E. Skipp, "*Of Time and the River*: The Final Editing," *Papers of the Bibliographical Society of America*, 64 (1970): 314–15; and James L. W. West III, "Fair Copy, Authorial Intention, and 'Versioning,'" *Text*, 6 (1994): 85–7. The standard biography of Perkins treats these matters; see A. Scott Berg, *Maxwell Perkins, Editor of Genius* (New York: E. P. Dutton, 1978).

passages, including the memorable description of Jay Gatsby's smile in Chapter III.

He fretted about the title as well. Throughout the making of the novel, Fitzgerald had difficulty deciding what to call it. Besides "The Great Gatsby," he considered "Among the Ash Heaps and Millionaires," "Trimalchio," "Trimalchio in West Egg," "On the Road to West Egg," "Gold-hatted Gatsby," and "The High-bouncing Lover." "Trimalchio," the title he almost chose for the published book, was the name of the ostentatious party-giver in the *Satyricon* of Petronius.[7]

The typescript that Fitzgerald mailed to Perkins in late October was apparently entitled "The Great Gatsby" – though no title page survives to prove it. By early November, Fitzgerald was instructing Perkins in a letter to call the novel "Trimalchio in West Egg." This was probably the title that Perkins sent to the Scribner Press; the typeset line at the head of each surviving galley reads "Fitzgerald's Trimalchio." On 18 November, however, Perkins reported to Fitzgerald that his fellow editors at Scribners did not like "Trimalchio in West Egg." Could the author supply another title? "I'll try my best but I don't know what I can do," Fitzgerald wrote back. "Maybe simply 'Trimalchio' or 'Gatsby.'"[8] In mid-December he instructed Perkins by cable to call the book "The Great Gatsby," but he continued to waver, suggesting "Gold-hatted Gatsby" and "Under the Red, White and Blue" in later communications. Three weeks before publication he remained dissatisfied: "I feel *Trimalchio* might have been best after all," he wrote.[9] By then, however, Perkins had told him that the title must stand. The novel had been sold in advance to the trade as *The Great Gatsby*; that would be its name.

Fitzgerald had been on the move while working on the galleys. He had returned the master proofs to Perkins in two batches, mailed separately on 24 January, from Rome, and 18 February, from Capri. (He retained the working proofs on which he had initially inscribed his revisions; this set survives today in his papers

---

[7] For information about Trimalchio in the *Satyricon*, see Appendix 2 of this edition.

[8] Fitzgerald to Perkins, *c.* 1 December 1924, *Dear Scott/Dear Max*, p. 85.

[9] Fitzgerald to Perkins, *c.* 12 March 1925, *Dear Scott/Dear Max*, p. 96.

at Princeton.)[10] There was not enough time for Fitzgerald to see and mark page proofs if his novel were to be ready for the spring selling season, so Perkins had the revises checked separately by two different readers at Scribners, and he read them himself. A courtesy set of page proofs went to Fitzgerald, but these do not survive. The first edition of the novel, in its revised form, with the title *The Great Gatsby*, was formally published on 10 April 1925.

The book has since become famous. Indeed, it is probably the most widely read novel written by an American in the twentieth century. *Trimalchio*, however, is virtually unknown. Besides Fitzgerald and Zelda, Perkins and his wife, a few members of the Scribners firm, and a handful of literary scholars, no one has ever read it. *Trimalchio* is not the same novel as *The Great Gatsby*. They are similar: the first two chapters of both books are almost identical; both novels have nine chapters and are narrated by Nick Carraway; both explore the effects of money and social class on human behavior and morality. The green light stands at the end of the Buchanans' dock in both novels; Dan Cody and Meyer Wolfshiem are in both texts; Jay Gatsby gives his fabulous parties and uses the term "old sport" in both narratives. *Trimalchio* and *Gatsby* both include the famous guest list for Gatsby's parties, and there is money in Daisy's voice in both novels.

There are crucial differences, however. Chapters VI and VII of *Trimalchio*, as noted, are almost entirely different from the corresponding chapters in *Gatsby*; elsewhere *Trimalchio* contains several lengthy passages that do not appear in *Gatsby*. Nick Carraway is not the same in *Trimalchio*: he is not quite so likable or self-deprecating, and he more obviously controls the narrative. His love affair with Jordan Baker is traced in greater detail, and we see more readily why they are attracted to each other. Jordan's character is more fully drawn; she and Nick are more clearly complicit in Daisy's affair with Gatsby, and in the wreckage that follows. The reader is more aware in *Trimalchio* of Gatsby's courting of celebrities – and of Tom and Daisy's aversion to them. The

---

[10] These galleys have been reproduced photographically in vol. III of *F. Scott Fitzgerald Manuscripts*, ed. Matthew J. Bruccoli (New York: Garland, 1990).

confrontation between Tom and Gatsby in the Plaza is handled differently in *Trimalchio* (Gatsby is less convincingly defeated), and the mechanics of moving the characters from Long Island to central Manhattan are managed in a less roundabout way.

Most importantly, the unfolding of Jay Gatsby's character is timed and executed in a wholly different fashion in *Trimalchio*. He remains shadowy and indistinct for a longer time; he gives Nick a few hints about his background, but not many. His past is a mystery until after Daisy runs down Myrtle Wilson while driving his yellow car. Some hours later, distraught and exhausted, Gatsby reveals his past to Nick in a beautifully rendered early-morning conversation – a sort of confessional scene. In a novel as intricately patterned and skillfully written as this one, all of these differences matter.

There is a tradition in Fitzgerald studies that *The Great Gatsby* became a masterpiece in revision. This edition of *Trimalchio* does not challenge that opinion.[11] Fitzgerald improved the novel in galleys; *The Great Gatsby* is a better book than *Trimalchio*. But *Trimalchio* is itself a remarkable achievement, and different enough from *Gatsby* to deserve publication on its own. It is now put into play, not only for comparison with *The Great Gatsby* but for interpretation as a separate and distinct work of art.

2. EDITORIAL PRINCIPLES

The text of *Trimalchio* survives in two identical sets of galley proofs – the working set marked by Fitzgerald, which is housed in his papers at Princeton University Library, and a clean set in the Department of Rare Books and Special Collections, Thomas Cooper Library, University of South Carolina. The printed texts of these two sets of galleys are the same; the South Carolina galleys are unmarked duplicates of the Princeton galleys.[12] The printed

---

[11] The edition also does not question the validity of Perkins' criticisms, though readers might wish to do so, now that the text which Perkins was criticizing – *Trimalchio*, not *The Great Gatsby* – can be read.

[12] The editor of this volume was allowed initially to inspect the South Carolina galleys only for two days, 14–15 August 1996. There was not time for a full

text of the Princeton galleys has been used as the basis for this edition of *Trimalchio*. A holograph manuscript also survives in the Princeton archive; its importance to this edition will be treated below in the discussion of accidentals.

Of the surviving texts, the galleys are nearest in substantive form to the typescript that Fitzgerald mailed to Scribners in October 1924. That typescript, which must perforce have served as setting copy for the galleys, does not survive. Perhaps it was returned to Fitzgerald with his sets of proofs; more likely it stayed at Scribners and was later discarded. In all probability Perkins made no verbal changes in this typescript. He was not an aggressive line editor; he rarely made revisions "within the sentence" for Fitzgerald or for any of his other authors.[13] Thus the galleys are probably, in substantive form, very close to the lost typescript, and in any case are as close as the surviving evidence will allow us to come to its text.

Accidentals are another matter. The copy-editors and compositors at Scribners surely made numerous changes in the spelling, punctuation, and word division of the typescript before setting its text in type, just as they had done for Fitzgerald's previous five books with the publisher. Scribners had a house style which was imposed on nearly every book it issued. That style can readily be detected in the galleys of this novel; it is also evident in the first editions of Hemingway, Wolfe, and other Scribners authors of the period. This was a quasi-British style of orthography and pointing, imposed so that unbound sheets or duplicate printing plates of Scribners books could be sent to British publishers. These publishers would then not have to reset the texts themselves – an important point dictated by U.S. and British copyright law of the

collation; the editor therefore compared the first word of each typeset line of text in the South Carolina galleys with the first word in each line of a photographic reproduction of the Princeton galleys. All first words of all lines were identical. In letterpress typesetting such evidence normally indicates that the entire texts are identical. In October 1999, the editor was allowed to perform a full hand collation of the South Carolina galleys against a facsimile of the marked Princeton galleys. The typeset texts proved to be indentical in every respect.

[13] This is true even for Wolfe, the writer with whom Perkins had the closest collaboration. Perkins' method with Wolfe was to suggest large cuts and re-arrangements of material but almost never to revise the actual prose.

time.[14] This is what happened for *Gatsby*; the first British "edition" of the novel is in fact an impression made from duplicates or molds of the Scribners second-printing plates that had been shipped to the British publisher, Chatto and Windus.[15]

The Scribners house style is alien to Fitzgerald's prose. In his handwritten drafts he did not use such forms as "to-day," "upstairs," "clew," "scepticism," "centre," "programme," or "criticise." His own pointing was much more free and open than the Scribners style, which involved heavy imposition of commas and creation of numerous hyphenated compounds. Fortunately this overlay of spelling and punctuation can be largely removed from the galley text by reference to the surviving holograph, which preserves the original texture of Fitzgerald's accidentals.[16] The holograph is not a fair copy from which the final typescript was prepared; rather, it is a composite document, representing more than one stage of composition. Still, it contains handwritten drafts of most of the passages in *Trimalchio*. Whenever possible, therefore, the spelling, punctuation, capitalization, and word division of this holograph have been used in this text, unless the holograph is demonstrably in error. Obvious typos or transcription errors in the galleys ("eyes" for "ice"; "oarden" for "garden") have been corrected.

A few features of the text of *Trimalchio* have been regularized to Fitzgerald's most common practice. Italics are reserved for emphasis; book, magazine, and newspaper titles are enclosed within quotation marks. Question marks and exclamation points following italicized words are also italicized. Dashes are one em within

---

[14] See the introduction to the Cambridge edition of *This Side of Paradise* (1995), ed. James L. W. West III, pp. xlix–l. Also see West, "The Chace Act and Anglo-American Literary Relations," *Studies in Bibliography*, 45 (1992): 303–12.

[15] This British impression, published by Chatto and Windus in 1926, prints all six plate variants introduced by Scribners for the second American trade printing. The Chatto impression bears the words "Printed in Great Britain" on the copyright page. Scribners almost surely shipped over duplicate second-printing plates, or molds of those plates, to the British printers. The originals would have been retained at Scribners in case subsequent American impressions were needed.

[16] This holograph has been reproduced photographically in THE GREAT GATSBY: *A Facsimile of the Manuscript*, ed. Matthew J. Bruccoli (Washington, D.C.: Microcard Editions Books, 1973).

sentences and two ems at the ends of sentences or fragments. Ellipsis points are normalized: three within sentences and four at the ends of sentences. The words "Sound" and "Park" – referring to Long Island Sound and Central Park – are capitalized. Fitzgerald's spellings of the names Wolfshiem and Epstien are permitted to stand. "East" and "West" as places are capitalized; "east" and "west" as directions are in lower case. (Fitzgerald was inconsistent, sometimes capitalizing the words and sometimes not, according to no discernible pattern.) Fitzgerald's preferred usage in the holograph – "middle-west" – is employed throughout.

The text of *Trimalchio* presented here leaves undisturbed a few factual irregularities that are present in the galleys. The only corrections made are for incongruities that Fitzgerald himself recognized and mended in his set of proofs. Other possible factual corrections are left unemended but are noted in a separate table in the apparatus. It is worth noting that most of the factual and chronological errors in the first edition of *The Great Gatsby* entered the text when Fitzgerald revised the galleys; thus they are not present in *Trimalchio*. The single sentence in *Trimalchio* requiring significant editorial emendation occurs in the fourth paragraph of the novel: "It was only Gatsby, the man who gives his name to this book, that was exempted from my reaction." Since this edition is entitled *Trimalchio*, the sentence has been emended to read: "It was only Gatsby who was exempted from my reaction."

Trimalchio is a notable literary achievement. It is a direct and straightforward narration of the story of Jay Gatsby, Nick Carraway, Jordan Baker, Myrtle and George Wilson, and Tom and Daisy Buchanan. The handling of plot details is surehanded; the writing is graceful and confident. *Trimalchio* will provide readers with new understanding of F. Scott Fitzgerald's working methods, fresh insight into his creative imagination, and renewed appreciation of his genius.

TRIMALCHIO

Trimalchio

BY
F. SCOTT FITZGERALD

CHAPTER I

In my younger and more vulnerable years my father told me something that I've been turning over in my mind ever since.

"When you feel like criticizing any one," he said, "just remember that everybody in this world hasn't had the advantages that you've had."

He didn't say any more but we've always been unusually communicative in a reserved way and I understood that he meant a great deal more than that. In consequence I'm inclined to reserve all judgements, a habit that has opened up many curious natures to me and also made me the victim of not a few veteran bores. The abnormal mind is quick to detect and attach itself to this quality when it appears in a normal person, and so it came about that in college I was unjustly accused of being a politician, because I was privy to the secret griefs of wild, unknown men. Most of the confidences were unsought—frequently I have feigned sleep, preoccupation or a hostile levity when I realized by some unmistakable sign that an intimate revelation was quivering on the horizon—for the intimate revelations of young men or at least the terms in which they express them are usually plagiaristic and marred by obvious suppressions. Reserving judgements is a matter of infinite hope. I am still a little afraid of missing something if I forget that, as my father snobbishly suggested and I snobbishly repeat, a sense of the fundamental decencies is parcelled out unequally at birth.

And, after boasting this way of my tolerance, I come to the admission that it has a limit. Conduct may be founded on the hard rock or the wet marshes but after a certain point I don't care what it's founded on. When I came back from the East last autumn I felt that I wanted the world to be in uniform and at a sort of moral attention forever; I wanted no more riotous excursions with privileged glimpses into the human heart. It was only Gatsby who

was exempted from my reaction. Gatsby who represented everything for which I have an unaffected scorn. If personality is an
unbroken series of successful gestures, then there was something
gorgeous about him, some heightened sensitivity to the promises of
life, as if he were related to one of those intricate machines that
register earthquakes ten thousand miles away. This responsiveness
had nothing to do with that flabby impressionability which is
dignified under the name of the "creative temperament"—it was an
extraordinary gift for hope, a romantic readiness such as I have
never found in any other person and which it is not likely I shall
ever find again. No—Gatsby turned out all right at the end; it is
what preyed on Gatsby, what foul dust floated in the wake of his
dreams that temporarily closed out my interest in the abortive
sorrows and unjustified elations of men.

My family have been substantial, well-to-do people in this
middle-western city for three generations. The Carraways are
something of a clan and we have a tradition that we're descended
from the Dukes of Buccleuch, but the actual founder of my line
was my grandfather's brother who came here in fifty-one, sent a
substitute to the Civil War and started the wholesale hardware
business that my father carries on today.

I never saw this great-uncle but I'm supposed to look like him—
with special reference to the rather hard-boiled painting that hangs
in Father's office. I graduated from New Haven in 1915, just a
quarter of a century after my father, and a little later I participated
in that delayed Teutonic migration known as the Great War. I
enjoyed the counter-raid so thoroughly that I came back restless.
Instead of being the warm center of the world the middle-west now
seemed like the ragged edge of the universe—so I decided to go
east and learn the bond business. Everybody I knew was in the
bond business so I supposed it could support one more single man.
All my aunts and uncles talked it over as if they were choosing a
prep-school for me and finally said "Why—ye-es" with very grave,
hesitant faces. Father agreed to finance me for a year and after
various delays I came east, permanently, I thought, in the spring of
twenty-two.

The practical thing was to find rooms in the city but it was a warm season and I had just left a country of wide lawns and friendly trees, so when a young man at the office suggested that we take a house together in a commuting town it sounded like a great idea. He found the house, a weatherbeaten cardboard bungalow at eighty a month, but at the last minute the firm ordered him to Washington and I went out to the country alone. I had a dog, at least I had him for a few days until he ran away, and an old Dodge and a Finnish woman who made my bed and cooked breakfast and muttered Finnish wisdom to herself over the electric stove.

It was lonely for a day or so until one morning some man, more recently arrived than me, stopped me on the road.

"How do you get to the village?" he asked helplessly.

I told him. And as I walked on I was lonely no longer. I was a guide, a pathfinder, an original settler. He had casually conferred on me the freedom of the neighborhood.

And so with the sunshine and the great bursts of leaves growing on the trees—just like things grow in fast movies—I had that familiar conviction that life was beginning over again with the summer.

There was so much to read for one thing and so much fine health to be pulled down out of the young breath-giving air. I bought a dozen volumes on banking and money and investment securities and they stood on my shelf in red and gold like new money from the mint, promising to unfold the shining secrets that only Midas and Morgan and Rothschild knew. And I had the high intention of reading many other books besides. I was rather literary in college—one year I wrote a series of very solemn and obvious editorials for the Yale "News"—and now I was going to bring back all such things into my life and become again that most limited of all specialists, the "well-rounded" man. This isn't just an epigram—life is much better looked at from a single window, after all.

It was a matter of chance that I should have rented a house in one of the strangest communities in North America. It was on that slender riotous island which extends itself due east of New York and where there are, among other natural curiosities, two unusual formations of land. Twenty miles from the city a pair of enormous eggs, identical in contour and separated only by a courtesy bay, jut out into the most domesticated body of salt water in the Western hemisphere, the great wet barnyard of Long Island Sound. They are not perfect ovals—like the egg in the Columbus story they are both crushed flat at the contact end—but their physical resemblance must be a source of perpetual wonder to the gulls that fly overhead. To the earth dwellers a more interesting phenomenon is their dissimilarity in every particular except shape and size.

I lived at West Egg, the—well, the less fashionable of the two, though this is a most superficial tag to express the bizarre and not a little sinister contrast between them. My house was at the very tip of the egg, only fifty yards from the Sound, and squeezed between two huge places that rented for twelve or fifteen thousand a season. The one on my right was a colossal affair by any standard—it was a factual imitation of some Hôtel de Ville in Normandy, with a tower on one side, spanking new under a thin beard of raw ivy, and a marble swimming pool and more than forty acres of lawn and garden. It was Gatsby's mansion. Or rather, as I didn't know Mr. Gatsby it was a mansion inhabited by a gentleman of that name. My own house was an eye-sore, but it was a small eye-sore and it had been overlooked, so I had a view of the water, a partial view of my neighbor's lawn and the consoling proximity of millionaires—all for eighty dollars a month.

Across the courtesy bay the white palaces of fashionable East Egg glittered along the water. The history of the summer really begins on the evening I drove over there to have dinner with the Tom Buchanans. Daisy was my second cousin once removed and I'd known Tom in college. And once just after the war I spent two days with them in Chicago.

Her husband, among various physical accomplishments, had been one of the most powerful ends that ever played football at New Haven—a national figure in a way, one of those men that reach such an acute limited excellence at twenty that everything afterwards savours of anti-climax. His family were enormously wealthy—even in college his spending capacity was a matter of scandal—but now he'd left Chicago and come east in a fashion that rather took your breath away: for instance he'd brought down a string of polo ponies from Lake Forest. It was hard to realize that a man in my own generation was wealthy enough to do that.

Why they came east I don't know. They had spent a year in France, for no particular reason, and then drifted here and there unrestfully wherever people played polo and were rich together. This was a permanent move said Daisy over the telephone, but I didn't believe it—I had no sight into Daisy's heart but I felt that Tom would drift on forever seeking a little wistfully for the dramatic turbulence of some irrecoverable football game.

And so it happened that on a warm windy evening I drove over to East Egg to see two old friends whom I scarcely knew at all. Their house was even more elaborate than I expected, a cheerful red and white Georgian Colonial mansion overlooking the bay. The lawn started at the beach and ran toward the front door for a quarter of a mile, jumping over sun-dials and brick walks and burning gardens—finally when it reached the house drifting up the side in bright vines as though from the momentum of its run. The front was broken by a line of French windows, glowing now with reflected gold, and wide open to the warm windy afternoon, and Tom Buchanan in riding clothes was standing with his legs apart on the front porch.

He had changed since his New Haven years. Now he was a sturdy, straw haired man of thirty with a rather hard mouth and a supercilious manner. Two shining, arrogant eyes had established dominance over his face and gave him the appearance of always leaning aggressively forward. Not even the effeminate swank of his riding clothes could hide the enormous power of that body—he seemed to fill those glistening boots until he strained the top lacing and you could see a great pack of muscle shifting when his shoulder moved under his thin coat. It was a body capable of enormous leverage—a cruel body.

His speaking voice, a gruff husky tenor, added to the impression of fractiousness he conveyed. There was a touch of paternal contempt in it, even toward people he liked—and there were men at New Haven who had hated his guts.

"Now, don't think my opinion on these matters is final," he

seemed to say, "just because I'm stronger and more of a man than you are." We were in the same Senior Society and while we were never intimate I always had the impression that he approved of me and wanted me to like him with some harsh, defiant wistfulness of his own.

We talked for a few minutes on the sunny porch.

"I've got a nice place here," he said, his eyes flashing about restlessly.

Turning me around with one arm he moved a broad flat hand along the front vista, including in its sweep a sunken Italian garden, a half acre of deep pungent roses and a snub-nosed motor-boat that bumped the tide off shore.

"It belonged to Demaine the oil man." He turned me around again, politely and abruptly. "We'll go inside."

We walked through a high hallway into a bright rosy-colored space, fragilely bound into the house by French windows at either end. The windows were ajar and gleaming white against the fresh grass outside that seemed to grow a little way into the house. A breeze blew through the room, blew curtains in at one end and out the other like pale flags, twisting them up toward the frosted wedding cake of the ceiling—and then rippled over the wine-colored rug, making a shadow on it as wind does on the sea.

The only completely stationary object in the room was an enormous couch on which two young women were buoyed up as though upon an anchored balloon. They were both in white and their dresses were rippling and fluttering as if they had just been blown back in after a short flight around the house. I must have stood for a few moments listening to the whip and snap of the curtains and the groan of a picture on the wall. Then there was a boom as Tom Buchanan shut the rear windows and the caught wind died out about the room and the curtains and the rugs and the two young women ballooned slowly to the floor.

The younger of the two women I had never seen. She was extended full length at her end of the divan, completely motionless and with her chin raised a little as if she were balancing something on it which was quite likely to fall. If she saw me out of the corner of her eyes she gave no hint of it—indeed I was almost surprised into murmuring an apology for having disturbed her by coming in.

The other girl, Daisy, made an attempt to rise—she leaned slightly forward with a conscientious expression—then she laughed, an absurd, charming little laugh, and I laughed too and came forward into the room.

"I'm p-paralyzed with happiness."

She laughed again as if she said something very witty and held my hand for a moment, looking up into my face, promising that there was no one in the world she so much wanted to see. That was a way she had. She hinted in a murmur that the surname of the balancing girl was Baker.

I've heard it said that Daisy's murmur was only to make people lean toward her; an irrelevant criticism that made it no less charming.

At any rate Miss Baker's lips fluttered, she nodded at me almost imperceptibly and then quickly tipped her head back again—the object she was balancing had obviously tottered a little and given her something of a fright. Again a sort of apology arose to my lips. Almost any exhibition of complete self sufficiency draws a stunned tribute from me.

I looked back at my cousin who began to ask me questions in her low, thrilling voice. It was the kind of voice that the ear follows up and down as if each speech is an arrangement of notes that will never be played again. Her face was sad and lovely with bright things in it, bright eyes and a bright passionate mouth—but there was an excitement in her voice that men who had cared for her found difficult to forget: a singing compulsion, a whispered "Listen," a promise that she had done gay exciting things just a while since and that there were gay, exciting things hovering in the next hour.

I told her how I had stopped off in Chicago for a day on my way east and how a dozen people had sent their love through me.

"Do they miss me?" she cried excitedly.

"The whole town is desolate. All the cars have the left rear wheel painted black as a mourning wreath and there's a persistent wail all night along the North Shore."

"How gorgeous! Let's go back, Tom. Tomorrow!" Then she added irrelevantly, "You ought to see the baby."

"I'd like to."

"She's asleep. She's three years old. Haven't you ever seen her?"

"Never."

"Well, you ought to see her. She's——"

Tom Buchanan who had been hovering restlessly about the room stopped and rested his hand on my shoulder.

"What you doing, Nick?"

"I'm a bond man."

"Who with?"

I told him.

"Never heard of them," he remarked decisively.

This annoyed me.

"You will," I answered shortly. "You will if you stay in the East."

"Oh, I'll stay in the East, don't you worry," he said, glancing at Daisy and then back at me as if he were alert for something more. "I'd be a God Damn fool to live anywhere else."

At this point Miss Baker said "Absolutely!" with such suddenness that I started—it was the first word she had uttered since I came into the room. Evidently it surprised her as much as it did me, for she yawned and with a series of rapid, deft movements stood up into the room.

"I'm stiff," she complained. "I've been lying on that sofa for as long as I can remember."

"Don't look at me," Daisy retorted. "I've been trying to get you to New York all afternoon."

"No thanks," said Miss Baker to the four cocktails just in from the pantry. "I'm absolutely in training."

Her host looked at her incredulously.

"You are!" He took down his drink as if it were a drop in the bottom of a glass. "How you ever get anything done is beyond me."

I looked at Miss Baker wondering what it was she "got done." I enjoyed looking at her. She was a slender, small-breasted girl with an erect carriage which she accentuated by throwing her body backward at the shoulders like a young cadet. Her grey sun-strained eyes looked back at me with polite reciprocal curiosity out of a wan, charming, discontented face. It occurred to me now that I had seen her, or a picture of her, somewhere before.

"You live in West Egg," she remarked contemptuously. "I know somebody there."

"I don't know a single——"

"You must know Gatsby."

"Gatsby?" demanded Daisy. "What Gatsby?"

Before I could reply that he was my neighbor dinner was announced; wedging his tense arm imperatively under mine Tom Buchanan compelled me from the room as though he were moving a checker to another square.

Slenderly, languidly, their hands set lightly on their hips the two young women preceded us out onto a rosy-colored porch open toward the sunset where four candles flickered on the table in the diminished wind.

"Why *candles?*" objected Daisy frowning. She snapped them out with her fingers. "In two weeks it'll be the longest day in the year." She looked at us all radiantly. "Do you always watch for the longest day of the year and then miss it? I always watch for the longest day of the year and then miss it."

"We ought to plan something," yawned Miss Baker, sitting down at the table as if she were getting into bed.

"All right," said Daisy. "What'll we plan?" She turned to me helplessly, "What do people plan?"

Before I could answer, her eyes fastened with an awed expression on her little finger.

"Look!" she exclaimed. "I hurt it."

We all looked—the knuckle was black and blue.

"You did it, Tom," she said accusingly. "I know you didn't mean to but you *did* do it. That's what I get for marrying a brute of a man, a great big hulking physical specimen of a——"

"Rain tomorrow," said Miss Baker raising her eyebrows at the scalloped sky. "Want to bet twenty-five on that, Tom?"

"I'll bet you seven dollars," said Daisy. "That's what Tom owes me, the great big hulking——"

"I hate that word hulking," objected Tom crossly, "even in kidding."

"Hulking," insisted Daisy.

Sometimes she and Miss Baker talked at once, unobtrusively and with a bantering inconsequence that was never quite chatter, that was as cool as their white dresses and their impersonal eyes in the absence of all desire. They were here—and they accepted Tom and me, making only a polite pleasant effort to entertain or to be entertained. They knew that presently dinner would be over and a little later the evening too would be over and casually put away. It was sharply different from the West where an evening was hurried from phase to phase toward its close in a continually disappointed anticipation or else in sheer nervous dread of the moment itself.

"You make me feel uncivilized, Daisy," I confessed on my second glass of wine. "Can't you talk about crops or something?"

I meant nothing in particular by this remark but it was taken up in an unexpected way.

"Civilization's going to pieces," broke out Tom violently. "I've gotten to be a terrible pessimist about things. Have you read 'The Rise of the Coloured Empires' by this man Goddard?"

"Why, no," I answered, rather surprised by his tone.

"Well, it's a fine book and everybody ought to read it. The idea is if we don't look out the white race will be—will be utterly submerged. It's all scientific stuff; it's been proved."

"Tom's getting very profound," said Daisy with an expression of unthoughtful sadness. "He reads deep books with long words in them. What was that word we——"

"Well, these books are all scientific," insisted Tom, glancing at her impatiently. "This fellow has worked out the whole thing. It's up to us who are the dominant race to watch out or these other races will have control of things."

"We've got to beat them down," whispered Daisy, winking solemnly toward the fervent sun.

"You ought to live in California——" began Miss Baker but Tom interrupted her by shifting heavily in his chair.

"This idea is that we're Nordics. I am and you are and you are and——" After an infinitesimal hesitation he included Daisy with a slight nod and she winked at me again, "—and we've produced all the things that go to make civilization—oh, science and art and all that, do you see?"

There was something pathetic in his concentration as if his complacency, more acute than of old, was not enough to him any more. When, almost immediately, the telephone rang inside and the butler left the porch Daisy seized upon the momentary interruption and leaned toward me.

"I'll tell you a family secret," she whispered enthusiastically. "It's about the butler's nose. Do you want to hear about the butler's nose?"

"That's what I came over for tonight."

"Well, he wasn't always a butler; he used to be the silver polisher for some people in New York that had a silver service for two hundred people. He had to polish it from morning till night until finally it began to affect his nose——"

"Things went from bad to worse," suggested Miss Baker.

"Yes. Things went from bad to worse until finally he had to give up his position."

For a moment the last sunshine fell with romantic affection upon her glowing face; her voice compelled me forward breathlessly as I listened—then the glow faded, each light deserting her with lingering regret like children leaving a pleasant street at dusk.

The butler came back and murmured something close to Tom's ear whereupon Tom frowned, pushed back his chair and without a word went inside. As if his absence quickened something within her Daisy leaned forward again, her voice glowing and singing.

"I love to see you at my table Nick. You remind me of a—of a rose, an absolute rose. Doesn't he?" She turned to Miss Baker for confirmation. "An absolute rose?"

This was untrue. I am not even faintly like a rose. She was only extemporizing but a stirring warmth flowed from her as if her heart was trying to come out to you concealed in one of those breathless, thrilling words. Then suddenly she threw her napkin on the table and excused herself and went into the house.

Miss Baker and I exchanged a short glance consciously devoid of meaning. I was about to speak when she sat up alertly and said "Sh!" in a warning voice. A subdued impassioned murmur was audible in the room beyond and Miss Baker leaned forward, unashamed, trying to hear. The murmur trembled on the verge of coherence, sank down, mounted excitedly and then ceased altogether.

"This Mr. Gatsby you spoke of is my neighbor——" I began.

"Don't talk. I want to hear what happens."

"Is something happening?" I inquired innocently.

"Do you mean to say you don't know?" said Miss Baker, honestly surprised. "I thought everybody knew."

"I don't."

"Why—" she said hesitantly, "Tom's got some woman in New York."

"Got some woman?" I repeated blankly.

Miss Baker nodded.

"She might have the decency not to telephone him at dinner-time. Don't you think?"

Almost before I had grasped her meaning there was the flutter of a dress and the crunch of leather boots and Tom and Daisy were back at the table.

"It couldn't be helped!" cried Daisy with tense gayety.

She sat down, glanced searchingly at Miss Baker and then at me and continued, "I looked outdoors for a minute and it's very romantic outdoors. There's a bird on the lawn that I think must be a nightingale come over on the Cunard or White Star Line. He's singing away—" her voice sang "—It's romantic. Isn't it, Tom?"

"Very romantic," he said, and then miserably to me: "If it's light enough after dinner I want to take you down to the stables."

The telephone rang inside, startlingly, and as Daisy shook her head decisively at Tom the subject of the stables, in fact all subjects, vanished into air. Among the broken fragments of the last five minutes at table I remember the candles being lit again, pointlessly, and I was conscious of wanting to look squarely at everyone and yet to avoid all eyes. I couldn't guess what Daisy and Tom were thinking but I doubt if even Miss Baker who seemed to have mastered a certain hardy skepticism was able utterly to put this fifth guest's shrill metallic urgency out of mind. To a certain temperament the situation might have seemed intriguing—my own instinct was to telephone immediately for the police.

The horses, needless to say, were not mentioned again. Tom and Miss Baker, with several feet of twilight between them, strolled back into the library, as if to a vigil beside a perfectly tangible body, while, trying to look pleasantly interested and a little deaf, I followed Daisy around a chain of connecting verandas to the porch in front. In its deep gloom we sat down side by side on a wicker settee.

Daisy took her face in her hands, as if feeling its lovely shape, and her eyes moved gradually out into the velvet dusk. I saw that turbulent emotions possessed her, so I asked what I thought would be some sedative questions about her little girl.

"We don't know each other very well, Nick," she said suddenly. "Even if we are cousins. You didn't come to my wedding."

"I wasn't back from the war."

"That's true." She hesitated. "Well, I've had a very bad time, Nick, and I'm pretty cynical about everything."

Evidently she had reason to be. I waited but she didn't say any more, and after a moment I returned rather feebly to the subject of her daughter.

"I suppose she talks, and—eats, and everything."

"Oh, yes," she replied absently. "Listen, Nick, let me tell you what I said when she was born. Would you like to hear?"

"Very much."

"It'll show you how I've gotten to feel about—things. Well, she was less than an hour old and Tom was God knows where. I woke up out of the ether with an utterly abandoned feeling and asked the nurse right away if it was a boy or a girl. She told me it was a girl, and so I turned my head away and wept. 'All right,' I said, 'I'm glad it's a girl. And I hope she'll be a fool—that's the best thing a girl can be in this world, a beautiful little fool.'

"You see I think everything's terrible anyhow," she went on in a convinced way. "Everybody thinks so—the most advanced people. And I know. I've been everywhere and seen everything and done everything." Her eyes flashed around her in a defiant way, rather like Tom's, and she laughed with thrilling scorn. "Sophisticated— God, I'm sophisticated!"

The instant her voice broke off, ceasing to compel my attention, my belief, I felt the basic insincerity of what she had said. It made me uneasy, as though the whole evening had been a trick of some sort to exact a contributary emotion from me. I waited, and sure enough, in a moment she looked at me with an absolute smirk on her lovely face as if she had asserted her membership in a rather distinguished secret society to which she and Tom belonged.

Inside, the crimson room bloomed with light. Tom and Miss Baker sat at either end of the long couch and she read aloud to him from the "Saturday Evening Post"—the words, murmurous and uninflected, running together in a soothing tune. The lamp-light, bright on his boots and dull on the autumn-leaf yellow of her hair, glinted along the paper as she turned a page with a flutter of slender muscles in her golden arms.

When we came in she held us silent for a moment with her lifted hand.

"To be continued," she said, tossing the magazine on the table, "in our very next issue."

Her body asserted itself with a restless movement of her knee, and she stood up.

"Ten o'clock," she remarked, apparently finding the time on the ceiling. "Time for this good girl to go to bed."

"Jordan's going to play in the tournament tomorrow," explained Daisy, "over at Westchester."

"Oh, you're Jordan Baker."

I knew now why her face was familiar—its pleasing contemptuous expression had looked out at me from many rotogravure pictures of the sporting life at Asheville and Hot Springs and Palm Beach. I had heard some story of her too, a critical, unpleasant story, but what it was I had forgotten long ago.

"Good night," she said softly. "Wake me at eight, won't you."

"If you'll get up."

"I will. Good night, Mr. Carraway. See you anon."

"Of course you will," confirmed Daisy. "In fact I think I'll arrange a marriage. Come over often, Nick, and I'll sort of—oh—fling you together. You know, lock you up accidentally in linen closets and push you out to sea in a boat, and all that sort of thing——"

"Good night!" called Miss Baker from the stairs. "I haven't heard a word."

"She's a nice girl," said Tom after a minute. "They oughtn't to let her run around the country this way."

"Who oughtn't to?" inquired Daisy coldly.

"Her family."

"Her family is one aunt about a thousand years old. Besides, Nick's going to look after her, aren't you, Nick? She's going to spend lots of week ends out here this summer. I think the home influence will be very good for her."

Daisy and Tom looked at each other for a moment in silence.

"Is she from New York?" I asked quickly.

"From Louisville. Our white girlhood was passed together there. Our beautiful white——"

"Did you give Nick a little heart-to-heart talk on the veranda?" demanded Tom suddenly.

"Did I?" She looked at me. "I can't seem to remember, but I think we talked about the Nordic race. Yes, I'm sure we did. It sort of crept up on us and first thing you know——"

"Don't believe everything you hear, Nick," he advised me.

I said lightly that I had heard nothing at all and a few minutes later I got up to go home. They came to the door with me and stood side by side in a cheerful square of light while I got into my car. As I started the motor Daisy peremptorily called "Wait!

"I forgot to ask you something, and it's important. We heard you were engaged to a girl out West."

"That's right," corroborated Tom kindly. "We heard that you were engaged."

"It's a libel. I'm too poor."

"But we heard it," insisted Daisy, surprising me by opening up again in a flower-like way. "We heard it from three people so it must be true."

Of course I knew what they were referring to, but I wasn't even vaguely engaged. The fact that the citizenry were accusing me of it was one of the reasons I had come east. You can't stop going with an old friend on account of rumors and on the other hand I had no intention of being rumored into marriage.

Their interest rather touched me and made them less remotely rich—nevertheless I was confused and a little disgusted as I drove away. It seemed to me that the thing for Daisy to do was to rush out of the house, child in arms—but apparently there were no such intentions in her head. As for Tom the fact that he "had some woman in New York" was really less surprising than that he had been depressed by a book. Something was making him nibble at the edge of stale ideas as if his sturdy physical egotism wasn't enough for him any more.

Already it was deep summer on roadhouse roofs and in front of wayside garages where new red gas-pumps sat out in pools of light, and when I reached my estate at West Egg I ran the car under its shed and sat for a while on an abandoned grass roller in the yard. The wind had blown off leaving a loud bright night with wings beating in the trees and a persistent organ sound as the full bellows of the earth blew the frogs full of life. The shadow of a moving cat wavered across the moonlight and turning my head to watch it I saw that I was not alone—fifty feet away a figure had moved out from the shadow of my neighbor's mansion and was standing with his hands in his pockets regarding the silver pepper of the stars. Something in his leisurely movements and the secure position of his feet upon the lawn suggested that it was Mr. Gatsby himself— come out to determine what share was his of our local heavens.

I decided to call to him. Jordan Baker had mentioned him at dinner, and that would do for an introduction. But I didn't call to him for he gave a sudden intimation that he was content to be alone—he stretched out his arms toward the dark water in a curious way, and far as I was from him I could have sworn he was trembling. Involuntarily I glanced seaward—there was nothing to be seen except a single green light, minute and far away, that might have been the end of a dock. When I looked once more for Mr. Gatsby he had gone, and I was alone again in the unquiet darkness.

CHAPTER II

About half way between West Egg and New York the motor-road hastily joins the railroad and runs beside it for a quarter of a mile so as to shrink away from a certain desolate area of land. This is a valley of ashes—a fantastic farm where ashes grow like wheat into ridges and hills and grotesque gardens, where ashes take the forms of houses and chimneys and rising smoke and finally, with a transcendent effort, of ash-grey men who move dimly and already crumbling through the powdery air.

Occasionally a line of grey cars crawls along an invisible track, gives out a ghastly creak and comes to rest, and immediately the ash-grey men swarm up with leaden spades and stir up an impenetrable cloud which screens their obscure operations from your sight.

But above the grey land and the spasms of bleak dust which drift endlessly over it, you perceive, after a moment, the eyes of Dr. T. J. Eckleburg. The eyes of Dr. T. J. Eckleburg are blue and gigantic—their retinas are one yard high. They look out of no face but, instead, from a pair of enormous yellow spectacles which pass over a nonexistent nose. Evidently some wild wag of an oculist set them there to fatten his practice in the borough of Queens and then sank down himself into eternal blindness or forgot them and moved away. But his eyes, dimmed a little by many paintless days under sun and rain, brood on over the solemn dumping ground.

The valley of ashes is bounded on one side by a small foul river, and when the drawbridge is up to let boats through, the passengers on waiting trains can stare at the dismal scene for as long as half an hour. There is always a wait there of at least a minute and it was because of this that I first met Tom Buchanan's mistress.

The fact that he had one was insisted upon wherever he was known. His acquaintances resented the fact that he turned up in popular cafés with her and, leaving her at the table, sauntered about chatting with whomsoever he knew. Though I was curious to see her I had no desire to meet her—but I did. I went up to New York with Tom on the train one afternoon and when we stopped by the ashheaps he jumped to his feet and taking hold of my elbow literally forced me from the car.

"We're getting off!" he insisted. "I want you to meet my girl."

I think he'd tanked up a good deal at luncheon and his determination to have my company bordered on violence. The supercilious assumption was that on Sunday afternoon I had nothing better to do.

I followed him over a low white-washed fence and we walked back a hundred yards along the road under Dr. Eckleburg's persistent stare. The only building in sight was a small block of yellow brick sitting on the edge of the waste land, a sort of compact Main Street ministering to it and contiguous to absolutely nothing. One of the three shops it contained was for rent; another was an all-night restaurant approached by a trail of ashes; the third was a garage—Repairs. GEORGE B. WILSON. Cars Bought and Sold—and I followed Tom inside.

The interior was unprosperous and bare; the only car visible was the dust-covered wreck of a Ford which crouched in a dim corner. It had occurred to me that this shadow of a garage must be a blind and that sumptuous and romantic apartments were concealed overhead when the proprietor himself appeared in the door of an office, wiping his hands on a piece of waste. He was a blond, spiritless man, anaemic and faintly handsome. When he saw us a damp gleam of hope sprung into his light blue eyes.

"Hello Wilson, old man," said Tom, slapping him jovially on the shoulder. "How's business?"

"I can't complain," answered Wilson unconvincingly. "When are you going to sell me that car?"

"Next week. I've got my man working on it now."

"Works pretty slow, don't he?"

"No, he doesn't," said Tom coldly. "And if you feel that way about it maybe I'd better sell it somewhere else after all."

"I don't mean that," explained Wilson quickly. "I just meant——"

His voice faded off and Tom glanced impatiently around the garage. Then I heard footsteps on a stairs and in a moment the thickish figure of a woman blocked out the light from the office door. She was in the middle thirties, and faintly stout, but she carried her flesh sensuously as some women can. Her face, above a soiled dress of dark blue crêpe-de-chine, contained no facet or gleam of beauty but there was an immediately perceptible vitality about her as if the nerves of her body were continually smouldering. She smiled slowly and walking through her husband as if he were a ghost shook hands with Tom, looking him flush in the eye. Then she wet her lips and without turning around spoke to her husband in a soft, coarse voice:

"Get some chairs, why don't you, so somebody can sit down."

"Oh sure," agreed Wilson hurriedly and went toward the little office, mingling immediately with the cement color of the walls. A white ashen dust veiled his dark suit and his yellow hair as it veiled everything in the vicinity—except his wife, who moved close to Tom.

"I want to see you," said Tom intently. "Get on the next train."

"All right."

"I'll meet you by the newsstand on the lower level."

She nodded and moved away from him just as George Wilson emerged with two chairs from his office door.

We waited for her down the road and out of sight. It was a few days before the Fourth of July, and a grey, scrawny Italian child was setting torpedoes in a row along the railroad track.

"Terrible place, isn't it," said Tom, exchanging a frown with Dr. Eckleburg.

"Awful."

"It does her good to get away."

"Doesn't her husband object?"

"Wilson? He thinks she goes to see her sister in New York. He's so dumb he doesn't know he's alive."

So Tom Buchanan and his girl and I went up together to New York—or not quite together, for Mrs. Wilson sat discreetly in another car. Tom Buchanan deferred that much to the sensibilities of those East Eggers who might be on the train.

She had changed her dress to a brown figured muslin which stretched tight over her rather wide hips as Tom helped her to the platform in New York. At the newsstand she bought a copy of "Town Tattle" and a moving picture magazine and, in the station drug store, some cold cream and a small flask of perfume. Upstairs in the solemn echoing drive she let four taxi cabs drive away before she selected a new one, lavender-colored with grey upholstery, and in this we slid out from the mass of the station into the glowing sunshine. But immediately she turned sharply from the window and leaning forward tapped on the front glass.

"I want to get one of those dogs," she said earnestly. "I want to get one for the apartment. They're nice to have, a dog."

We backed up to a grey old man who bore an absurd resemblance to John D. Rockefeller. In a basket, swung from his neck, cowered a dozen very recent puppies of an indeterminate breed.

"What kind are they?" asked Mrs. Wilson eagerly as he came to the taxi window.

"All kinds. What kind do you want, lady?"

"I'd like to get one of those police dogs. I don't suppose you got that kind?"

The man peered doubtfully into the basket, plunged in his hand and drew one up, wriggling, by the back of the neck.

"That's no police dog," said Tom.

"No, it's not exactly a *police* dog," said the man with disappointment in his voice. "It's more of an airedale." He passed his hand over the brown washrag of a back. "Look at that coat. Some coat. That's a dog that'll never bother you with catching cold."

"I think it's cute," said Mrs. Wilson enthusiastically. "How much is it?"

"That dog?" He looked at it admiringly. "*That* dog will cost you ten dollars."

The airedale—undoubtedly there was an airedale concerned in it somewhere though its feet were startlingly white—changed hands and settled down into Mrs. Wilson's lap where she fondled the weather-proof coat with rapture.

"Is it a boy or a girl?" she asked delicately.

"That dog? That dog's a boy."

"It's a bitch," said Tom decisively. "Here's your money. Go and buy ten more dogs with it."

We drove over to Fifth Avenue, warm and soft, almost pastoral on the summer Sunday afternoon. I wouldn't have been surprised to see a great flock of white sheep turn the corner.

"Hold on," I said. "I have to leave you here."

"No, you don't," interposed Tom quickly. "Myrtle'll be hurt if you don't come up to the apartment. Won't you, Myrtle?"

"Come on," she urged. "I'll telephone my sister Catherine. She's said to be very beautiful by people who ought to know."

"Well, I'd like to, but——"

We went on, cutting back again over the Park toward the West Hundreds. At 158th Street the cab stopped at one slice in a long white cake of apartment houses. Throwing a regal homecoming glance around the neighborhood, Mrs. Wilson gathered up her dog and her other purchases and went haughtily in.

"I'm going to have the McKees come down," she announced as we rose in the elevator. "And of course I got to call up my sister too."

The apartment was on the top floor—a small living room, a small dining room, a small bedroom and a bath. The living room was crowded to the doors with a set of tapestried furniture entirely too large for it so that to move about was to stumble continually over scenes of ladies swinging in the gardens of Versailles. The only picture was an over-enlarged photograph, apparently a hen sitting on a blurred rock. Looked at from a distance however the hen resolved itself into a bonnet and the countenance of a stout old lady beamed down into the room. Several old copies of "Town Tattle" lay on the table together with a copy of "Simon Called Peter" and some of the small scandal magazines of Broadway. Mrs. Wilson was first concerned with the dog. A reluctant elevator boy went for a box full of straw and some milk to which he added on his own initiative a tin of large hard dog biscuits—one of which decomposed apathetically in the saucer of milk all afternoon. Meanwhile Tom brought out a bottle of whiskey from a locked bureau door.

I have been drunk just twice in my life and the second time was that afternoon, so everything that happened has a dim hazy cast over it although until after eight o'clock the apartment was full of cheerful sun. Sitting on Tom's lap Mrs. Wilson called up several people on the telephone; then there were no cigarettes and I went out to buy some at the drug store on the corner. When I came back they had both disappeared so I sat down discreetly in the living room and read a chapter of "Simon Called Peter"—either it was terrible stuff or the whiskey distorted things because it didn't make any sense to me.

Just as Tom and Myrtle—after the first drink Mrs. Wilson and I called each other by our first names—reappeared, company commenced to arrive at the apartment door.

The sister, Catherine, was a slender, worldly girl of about thirty with a solid sticky bob of red hair and a complexion powdered milky white. Her eyebrows had been plucked and then drawn on again at a more rakish angle but the efforts of nature toward the restoration of the old alignment gave a blurred air to her face. When she moved about there was an incessant clicking as innumerable pottery bracelets jingled up and down upon her arms. She came in with such a proprietary haste and looked around so possessively at the furniture that I wondered if she lived here. But when I asked her she laughed immoderately, repeated my question aloud and told me she lived with a girl friend at a hotel.

Mr. McKee was a pale feminine man from the flat below. He had just shaved for there was a white spot of lather on his cheekbone and he was most respectful in his greeting to everyone in the room. He informed me that he was in the "artistic game" and I gathered later that he was a photographer and had made the dim enlargement of Mrs. Wilson's mother which hovered like an ectoplasm on the wall. His wife was shrill, languid, handsome and horrible. She told me with pride that her husband had photographed her a hundred and twenty-seven times since they had been married.

Mrs. Wilson had changed her costume some time before and was now attired in an elaborate afternoon dress of cream colored chiffon which gave out a continual rustle as she swept about the room. With the influence of the dress her personality had also undergone a change. Her intense vitality, that had been so remarkable in the garage, was converted into impressive hauteur. Her laughter, her gestures, her assertions became more violently affected moment by moment and as she expanded the room grew smaller around her until she seemed to be revolving on a noisy, creaking pivot through the smoky air.

"My dear," she told her sister in a high mincing shout, "most of these fellas will cheat you every time. All they think of is money. I had a woman up here last week to look at my feet and when she gave me the bill you'd of thought she had my appendix out."

"What was the name of the woman?" asked Mrs. McKee.

"Mrs. Eberhardt. She goes around looking at peoples' feet in their own homes."

"I like your dress," remarked Mrs. McKee. "I think it's adorable."

Mrs. Wilson rejected the compliment by raising her eyebrow in disdain.

"It's just a crazy old thing," she said. "I just slip it on sometimes when I don't care what I look like."

"But it looks wonderful *on* you, if you know what I mean," pursued Mrs. McKee. "If Chester could only get you in that pose I think he could make something of it."

We all looked in silence at Mrs. Wilson who removed a strand of hair from over her eyes and looked back at us with a radiant smile. Mr. McKee regarded her intently with his head on one side and then moved his hand back and forth slowly in front of his face.

"I should change the light," he said after a moment. "I'd like to bring out the modelling of the features. And I'd try to get hold of all the back hair."

"I wouldn't think of changing the light," cried Mrs. McKee. "I think it's——"

Her husband said "Sh!" and we all looked at the subject again whereupon Tom Buchanan yawned audibly and got to his feet.

"You McKees have something to drink," he said. "Get some more ice and mineral water, Myrtle, before everybody goes to sleep."

"I told that boy about the ice." Myrtle raised her eyebrows in despair at the shiftlessness of the lower orders. "These people! You have to keep after them all the time."

She looked at me and laughed pointlessly. Then she flounced over to the dog, kissed it with ecstasy and swept into the kitchen, implying that a dozen chefs awaited her orders there.

"I've done some nice things out on Long Island," asserted Mr. McKee.

Tom looked at him blankly.

"Two of them we have framed downstairs."

"Two what?" demanded Tom.

"Two studies. One of them I call 'Montauk Point—the Gulls' and the other I call 'Montauk Point—the Sea.'"

The sister Catherine sat down beside me on the couch.

"Do you live down on Long Island too," she inquired.

"I live at West Egg."

"Really? I was down there at a party about a month ago. At a man named Gatsby's. Do you know him?"

"I live next door to him."

"Well, they say he's a nephew or a cousin of Kaiser Wilhelm's. That's where all his money comes from."

"Really?"

She nodded.

"I'm scared of him. I'd hate to have him get anything on me."

This absorbing information about my neighbor was interrupted by Mrs. McKee's pointing suddenly at Catherine:

"Chester, I think you could do something with *her*," she broke out, but Mr. McKee only nodded in a bored way and turned his attention to Tom.

"I'd like to do more work on Long Island if I could get the entry. All I ask is that they should give me a start."

"Ask Myrtle," said Tom breaking into a short shout of laughter as Mrs. Wilson entered with a tray. "She'll give you a letter of introduction, won't you Myrtle?"

"Do what?" she asked startled.

"You'll give McKee a letter of introduction to your husband, so he can do some studies of him." His lips moved silently for a moment as he invented. "'George B. Wilson at the Gasoline Pump,' or something like that."

Catherine leaned close to me and whispered in my ear:

"Neither of them can stand the person they're married to."

"Can't they?"

"Can't *stand* them." She looked at Myrtle and then at Tom. "What I say is, why go on living with them if they can't stand them? If I was them I'd get a divorce and get married to each other right away."

"Doesn't she like Wilson either?"

The answer to this was unexpected. It came from Myrtle who had overheard the question and it was violent and obscene.

"You see?" cried Catherine triumphantly. She lowered her voice again. "It's really his wife that's keeping them apart. She's a Catholic and they don't believe in divorce."

Daisy was not a Catholic and I was a little shocked at the elaborateness of the lie.

"When they *do* get married," continued Catherine, "they're going west to live for awhile until it blows over."

"It'd be more discreet to go to Europe."

"Oh, do you like Europe?" she exclaimed surprisingly. "I just got back from Monte Carlo."

"Really."

"Just last year. I went over there with another girl."

"Stay long?"

"No, we just went to Monte Carlo and back. We went by way of Marseilles. We had over twelve hundred dollars when we started but we got gyped out of it all in two days in the private rooms. We had an awful time getting back, I can tell you. God, how I hated that town!"

The late afternoon sky bloomed in the window for a moment like the fairy blue of the Mediterranean—then the shrill voice of Mrs. McKee called me back into the room.

"I almost made a mistake too," she declared vigorously. "I almost married a little kyke who'd been after me for years. I knew he was below me. Everybody kept saying to me 'Lucille, that man's *way* below you!' But if I hadn't met Chester he'd of got me sure."

"Yes, but listen," said Myrtle Wilson, nodding her head up and down. "At least you didn't marry him."

"I know I didn't."

"Well, I married him," said Myrtle ambiguously. "And that's the difference between your case and mine."

"Why did you, Myrtle?" demanded Catherine. "Nobody forced you to."

Myrtle considered.

"I married him because I thought he was a gentleman," she said finally. "I thought he knew something about breeding but he wasn't fit to lick my shoe."

"You were crazy about him for awhile," said Catherine.

"Crazy about him?" cried Myrtle incredulously. "Who said I was crazy about him? I never was any more crazy about him than I was about that man there!"

She pointed suddenly at me and everyone looked at me accusingly. I tried to show by my expression that I expected no affection whatsoever.

"The only *crazy* I was was when I married him. I knew right away I made a mistake. He borrowed somebody's best suit to get married in, and never even told me about it. The man came after it one day when he was out: 'Oh, is that your suit?' I said. 'This is the first I ever heard about it.' But I gave it to him and then I lay down and cried to beat the band all afternoon."

"She really ought to get away from him," resumed Catherine to me. "They've been living over that garage for eleven years. And Tom's the first sweetie she ever had."

The bottle of whiskey—a second one—was now in constant motion. Tom rang for the janitor and sent him for some celebrated sandwiches which were a complete supper in themselves. I wanted to get out and walk eastward toward the park through the soft twilight but each time I tried to go I became entangled in some wild strident argument which pulled me back, as if with ropes, into my chair. But high over the city our line of yellow windows must have contributed their share of human secrecy to the casual watcher in the darkening streets; and I was him too, looking up and wondering. I was within and without, simultaneously enchanted and repelled by the inexhaustible variety of life.

Myrtle pulled her chair close to mine and suddenly her warm breath poured over me the story of her first meeting with Tom.

"It was on the two little seats facing each other that are always the last ones left on the train. I was going up to New York to see my sister and spend the night. He had on a dress suit and patent leather shoes and I couldn't keep my eyes off him but every time he looked at me I had to pretend to be looking at the advertisement over his head. When we came into the station he was next to me and his white shirt front pressed against my arm—and so I told him I'd have to call a policeman but he knew I lied. I was so excited that when I got into a taxi with him I didn't hardly know I wasn't getting into a subway train. All I kept thinking about over and over was 'You can't live forever, you can't live forever.'"

She turned to Mrs. McKee and the room rang full of her artificial laughter.

"My dear," she cried, "I'm going to give you this dress as soon as I'm through with it. I've got to get another one tomorrow. I'm going to make a list of all the things I've got to get. A massage and a wave and a collar for the dog and one of those cute little ash trays where you touch a spring, and a wreath with a black silk bow for mother's grave that'll last all summer. I got to write down a list so I won't forget all the things I got to do."

It was nine o'clock—almost immediately afterwards I looked at my watch and found it was ten. Mr. McKee was asleep on a chair with his fists clenched in his lap, like a photograph of a man of action. Taking out my handkerchief I wiped from his cheek the spot of dried lather that had worried me all the afternoon.

The little dog was sitting on the table looking with blind eyes through the smoke and from time to time groaning faintly. People disappeared, reappeared, made plans to go somewhere, and then lost each other, searched for each other, found each other a few feet away. Some time toward midnight Tom Buchanan and Mrs. Wilson stood face to face discussing in impassioned voices whether Mrs. Wilson had any right to mention Daisy's name.

"Daisy! Daisy! Daisy!" shouted Mrs. Wilson. "I'll say it whenever I want to! Daisy! Dai——"

Making a short deft movement Tom Buchanan broke her nose with his open hand.

Then there were bloody towels upon the bathroom floor and

women's voices scolding, and high over the confusions a long broken wail of pain. Mr. McKee awoke from his doze and started in a daze toward the door. When he had gone half way he turned around and stared at the scene—his wife and Catherine scolding and consoling as they stumbled here and there among the crowded furniture with articles of aid, and the despairing figure on the couch bleeding fluently and trying to spread a copy of "Town Tattle" over the tapestry scenes of Versailles. Then Mr. McKee turned and continued on out the door. Taking my hat from the chandelier I followed.

"Come to lunch some day," he suggested as we groaned down in the elevator.

"Where?"

"Anywhere."

"Keep your hands off the lever," said the elevator boy.

"I beg your pardon," said Mr. McKee with dignity. "I didn't know I was touching it."

"All right," I agreed, "I'll be glad to."

. . . I was standing beside his bed and he was sitting up between the sheets, still clad in his underwear, and with a great portfolio in his hands.

"Beauty and the Beast . . . Loneliness . . . Old Grocery Horse . . . Brook'n Bridge. . . ."

Then I was lying half asleep in the cold lower level of the Pennsylvania Station, staring at the morning "Tribune" and waiting for the four o'clock train.

CHAPTER III

There was music from my neighbor's house through the summer nights. In his blue gardens men and girls came and went like moths among the whisperings and the champagne and the stars. At high tide in the afternoon I watched his guests diving from the tower of his raft or taking the sun on the hot sand of his beach while his two motorboats slit the waters of the Sound, drawing aquaplanes over cataracts of foam. On week-ends his Rolls-Royce became an omnibus, bearing parties to and from the city, between nine in the morning and long past midnight, while his station wagon scampered like a brisk yellow bug to meet all trains. And on Mondays eight servants including an extra gardener toiled all day with mops and scrubbing-brushes and hammers and garden shears, repairing the ravages of the night before.

Every Friday three crates of oranges and lemons arrived from a fruiterer in New York—every Monday these same oranges and lemons left his back door in a pyramid of pulpless halves. There was a machine in the kitchen which could extract the juice of two hundred oranges in half an hour, if a little button was pressed two hundred times by a butler's thumb.

At least once a fortnight a corps of caterers came down with several hundred feet of canvas and enough colored lights to make a Christmas tree of Gatsby's enormous garden. On buffet tables, garnished with glistening hors d'oeuvre, spiced baked hams crowded against salads of harlequin designs and pastry pigs and turkeys bewitched to a dark gold. In the main hall a bar with a real brass rail was set up, and stocked with gins and liquors and with cordials so long forgotten that most of his female guests were too young to recognize their names.

By seven o'clock the orchestra has arrived—no thin five piece affair but a whole pitful of oboes and trombones and saxophones and viols and cornets and piccolos and low and high drums. The last swimmers have come in from the beach now and are dressing upstairs; the cars from New York are parked five deep in the drive, and already the halls and salons and verandas and gardens are gaudy with primary colors and hair bobbed in strange new ways and shawls beyond the dreams of Castile. The bar is in full swing and floating rounds of cocktails permeate the garden outside until the air is alive with chatter and laughter and casual innuendo and introductions forgotten on the spot and enthusiastic meetings between women who never knew each others' names.

The lights grow brighter as the earth lurches away from the sun and now the orchestra is playing yellow cocktail music and the opera of voices pitches a key higher. Laughter is easier, minute by minute, spilled with prodigality tipped out at a cheerful word. The groups change more swiftly, swell with new arrivals, dissolve and form in the same breath—already there are wanderers, confident girls who weave here and there among the stouter and more stable, become for a sharp, joyous moment the center of a group and then excited with triumph glide on through the sea-change of faces and voices and color under the constantly changing light.

Suddenly one of these gypsies in trembling opal seizes a cocktail out of the air, dumps it down for courage and moving her hands like Frisco dances out alone on the canvas platform. A momentary hush; the orchestra leader varies his rhythm obligingly for her and there is a burst of chatter as the erroneous news goes around that she is Gilda Gray's understudy from the Follies. The party has begun.

I believe that on the first night I went to Gatsby's house I was one of the few guests who had actually been invited. People were not invited—they went there. They got into automobiles which bore them out to Long Island and somehow they ended up at Gatsby's door. Once there they were introduced by somebody who knew Gatsby and after that they conducted themselves according to the rules of behavior associated with an amusement park. Sometimes they came and went without having met Gatsby at all, came for the party, with a simplicity of heart that was its own ticket of admission.

I had been actually invited. A chauffeur in a uniform of robin's egg blue crossed my lawn early that Saturday morning with a surprisingly formal note from his employer—the honor would be entirely Gatsby's, it said, if I would attend his "little party" that night. He had seen me several times and had intended to call on me long before but a peculiar combination of circumstances had prevented it—signed Jay Gatsby in a majestic hand.

Dressed up in white flannels I went over to his lawn a little after seven and wandered around rather ill-at-ease for half an hour among swirls and eddies of people I had never seen before. I tried to find my host but the two or three people of whom I asked his whereabouts stared at me in such an amazed way and denied so vehemently any knowledge of his movements that I slunk off in the direction of the cocktail table—the only place in the garden where a single man could linger without looking purposeless and alone.

I was on my way to get roaring drunk from sheer embarrassment when Jordan Baker came out of the house and stood at the head of the marble steps, leaning a little backward and looking with contemptuous interest down into the garden.

Welcome or not I found it necessary to attach myself to someone before I should begin to address cordial remarks to the passers-by.

"Hello!" I roared, advancing toward her. My voice seemed unnaturally loud across the garden.

She looked around.

"I thought you might be here," she responded. "I remembered you lived next door to——"

She took my arm, as a promise that she'd take care of me in a minute, and gave ear to two girls in twin yellow dresses who stopped at the foot of the steps.

"Hello!" they cried together. "Sorry you didn't win."

That was for the golf tournament. She had lost in the finals the week before.

"You don't know who we are," said one of the girls in yellow, "but we met you here about a month ago."

"You've dyed your hair since then," remarked Jordan and I started but the girls had moved casually on and were talking to an elaborate orchid of a woman who sat in state under a white plum tree.

"Do you see who that is?" asked Jordan.

Suddenly I did see, with that peculiarly unreal feeling which accompanied the recognition of a hitherto ghostly celebrity of the movies.

"The man with her is her director," she explained. "He's just been married. It's in all the movie magazines."

"Married to her?"

"No."

Then after another glance around:

"Look at all the young Englishmen."

There were over a dozen of them, all well dressed, all a little hungry, all talking in low earnest voices to moving picture magnates or bankers or anyone who might possibly buy insurance or automobiles or bonds or whatever the young Englishmen were trying to sell. They were agonizingly aware of the easy money in the vicinity and believed fondly that it was theirs for a few words in the right key.

It was still twilight but there was already a moon, produced no doubt like the supper out of a caterer's basket. With Jordan's slender golden arm resting in mine we went down the steps and sauntered about the garden. A tray of cocktails floated at us through the twilight and we sat down at a table with the two girls in yellow and three men, each one introduced to us as Mr. Mumble.

"Do you come to these parties often?" inquired Jordan of the girl beside her.

"The last one was the one I met you at," answered the girl in an alert, confident voice. She turned to her companion: "Wasn't it for you, Lucille?"

It was for Lucille too.

"I like to come," Lucille said. "I never care what I do, so I always have a good time. When I was here last I tore my gown on a chair, and he asked me my address—inside of a week I got a package from Croirier's with a new evening gown in it."

"Did you keep it?" asked Jordan.

"Sure I did. I was going to wear it tonight, but it was too big in the bust and had to be altered. It was grey with lavender beads. Two hundred and sixty-five dollars."

"There's something funny about a fellow that'll do a thing like that," volunteered the first girl. "He doesn't want any trouble with *any*body."

"Who doesn't?" I inquired.

"Gatsby. Somebody told me———"

The two girls and Jordan leaned together with an air of conspiracy.

"Somebody told me they thought he killed a man once."

A thrill passed over all of us. The three Mr. Mumbles bent forward and listened eagerly.

"I don't think it's so much *that*," argued Lucille skeptically; "it's more that he was a German spy during the war."

One of the men nodded in confirmation.

"I heard that from a man who knew all about him, grew up with him in Germany," he assured us frowning.

"Oh no," said the first girl, "it couldn't be that, because he was in the American army during the war." As our credulity switched back to her she leaned forward with enthusiasm. "You look at him sometime when he thinks nobody's looking at him. I'll *bet* he killed a man."

She narrowed her eyes and shivered. Lucille shivered. We all turned and looked around for Gatsby. It was a witness to the romantic speculation he inspired that there were whispers about him from those who had found little that it was necessary to whisper about in this world.

The first supper—there would be another one after midnight—was now being served and Jordan invited me to join her own party who were spread around a table on the other side of the garden. There were three married couples and Jordan's escort, a persistent undergraduate given to violent innuendo and obviously under the impression that sooner or later Jordan was going to yield him up her person to a greater or lesser degree. Instead of rambling this party had preserved a dignified homogeneity, and assumed to itself the function of representing the staid nobility of the country-side—

West Egg condescending to East Egg, and carefully on guard against its spectroscopic gayety.

The men—I had known one of them at New Haven—all affected the Oxford mush-mouth accent but, as I presently discovered, they were by no means snobs.

"Entering son Eton and Groton," remarked my friend. "Prob'ly send him Andovah, though. Wouldn't want him to turn out snob."

"Good idea," I suggested. "Why not send him to a high school in New York?"

He laughed.

"I've been out with those two girls you were talking to," announced the undergraduate to Jordan. "God how they do bore me!"

"Who?" she asked absently.

"Those two girls in yellow. I'd rather pass my afternoons in the glass parlors at Westover."

"That may be true," answered Jordan. "We may be the kind of girls you go around with, but those are the kind of girl you marry."

She put her plate on a chair and leaning back and smiling a wan smile regarded the dark open sky. At this table the conversation was turning upon the movie star. Someone had heard her refer to her legs as "limbs" and so they all laughed because they said legs and not limbs which put them at a big advantage. The women were more kind about her after they heard that she said limbs.

"Come on," whispered Jordan to me. "Let's get out."

We got up and she explained that we were going to find the host—I had never met him, she said, and it was making me uneasy. The undergraduate nodded in a cynical, melancholy way.

The bar, where we glanced first, was crowded but Gatsby was not there. She couldn't find him from the top of the steps, and he wasn't on the veranda. On a chance we tried an important-looking door and walked into a high gothic library panelled with carved English oak, and probably transported complete from some ruin overseas.

A stout, middle-aged man with enormous owl-eyed spectacles was sitting somewhat drunk on the edge of a great table, staring with unsteady concentration at the shelves of books. As we entered he wheeled excitedly around and examined Jordan from head to foot.

"What do you think?" he demanded impetuously.

"About what?"

He waved his hand toward the bookshelves.

"About that. As a matter of fact you needn't bother to as-ascertain. I ascertained. They're real."

"The books?"

He nodded.

"Absolutely real—have pages and everything. I thought they'd be a nice durable cardboard. Matter of fact they're absolutely real. Pages and—— Here! Lemme show you."

Taking our skepticism for granted he rushed to the bookcases and returned with Volume One of the "Stoddard Lectures."

"See?" he cried triumphantly. "It's a bona fide piece of printed matter. It fooled me. This fella's a regular Belasco. It's a triumph. What thoroughness! What realism! Knew when to stop too— didn't cut the pages. But what do you want? What do you expect?"

He snatched the book from me and replaced it hastily on its shelf muttering that if one brick was removed the whole library was liable to collapse.

"Who brought you?" he demanded. "Or did you just come? I was brought. Most people were brought."

Jordan looked at him alertly, cheerfully, without answering.

"I was brought by a woman named Roosevelt," he continued. "Mrs. Claud Roosevelt. Do you know her? I met her somewhere last night. I've been drunk for about a week now, and I thought it might sober me up to sit in a library."

"Has it?"

"A little bit, I think. I can't tell yet. I've only been here an hour. Did I tell you about the books? They're real. They're——"

"You told us."

We shook hands with him gravely and went back outdoors.

There was dancing now on the canvas in the garden, old men pushing young girls backward in eternal graceless circles, superior couples holding each other tortuously, fashionably, and keeping in the corners—and a great number of single girls dancing individualistic jazz or relieving the orchestra for a moment of the burden of the banjo or the traps.

"I love large parties," said Jordan. "They're so intimate. At small parties there isn't any privacy. You having a good time?"

"I'm having a good time with you."

At midnight the hilarity had increased. A celebrated tenor had sung in Italian and a notorious contralto had sung in jazz and between the numbers people were doing "stunts" all over the garden while happy vacuous bursts of laughter rose toward the summer sky. A pair of stage "twins"—who turned out to be the girls in yellow, did a baby act in costume and champagne was served in glasses bigger than finger bowls. The moon had risen higher, and floating in the Sound was a triangle of silver scales, trembling a little to the stiff, tinny drip of the banjoes on the lawn.

I was still with Jordan Baker. We were sitting at a table with a man of about my age and a rowdy little girl who gave away upon the slightest provocation to uncontrollable laughter. I was enjoying myself now. I had taken two finger bowls of champagne and the scene had changed before my eyes into something significant, elemental and profound.

At a lull in the entertainment the man looked at me and smiled.

"Your face is familiar," he said hesitantly. "Weren't you in the First Division during the war?"

"Why, yes. I was in the Twenty-eighth Infantry."

"I was in the Sixteenth until June, nineteen-eighteen. I knew I'd seen you somewhere before."

We talked for a moment about some wet, grey little villages in France. Evidently he lived in this vicinity for he told me that he had just bought a hydroplane and was going to try it out in the morning.

"Want to go with me, old sport? Just near the shore along the Sound."

"What time?"

"Any time that suits you best."

It was on the tip of my tongue to ask his name when Jordan looked around and smiled.

"Having a gay time now?" she inquired.

"Much better." I turned again to my new acquaintance. "This is an unusual party for me. I haven't even seen the host. I live over there——" I waved my hand at the invisible hedge in the distance, "and this man Gatsby sent over his chauffeur with an invitation."

For a moment he looked at me as if he failed to understand.

"I'm Gatsby," he said suddenly.

"What!" I exclaimed. "Oh, I beg your pardon."

"I thought you knew, old sport. I'm afraid I'm not a very good host."

He was only a little older than me—somehow I had expected a florid and corpulent person in his middle years—yet he was somehow not a young man at all. There was a stiff dignity about him, and a formality of speech that just missed being absurd, that always trembled on the verge of absurdity until you wondered why you didn't laugh. I got a distinct impression that he was picking his words with care.

Almost at the moment when he identified himself a butler hurried toward him with the information that Chicago was calling him on the wire. He excused himself with a bow and a polite smile that included each of us in turn.

"If you want anything just ask for it, old sport," he said. "Excuse me. I will rejoin you later."

When he was gone I turned immediately to Jordan, constrained to assure her that I rather liked him.

"He says he's an Oxford man," she remarked.

"Have you got some prejudice against Oxford?"

"I don't think he went there."

"Why not?"

"I don't know," she insisted. "I just don't think he did."

Something in her tone reminded me of the other girl's "I think he killed a man." Before I could discover the reason for her disbelief the gigantic orchestra leader tapped his stand imperatively and after some moments was rewarded by a rough caricature of silence.

"Ladies and gentlemen," he began. "At the request of Mr. Gatsby we are going to play for you Mr. Vladimir Epstien's latest work which attracted so much attention at Carnegie Hall last May.

If you read the papers you know there was a big sensation." He smiled with jovial condescension and added "Some sensation!" whereupon everybody laughed.

"The piece is known," he concluded lustily, "as 'Vladimir Epstien's Jazz History of the World.'"

When he sat down the members of the orchestra looked at one another and smiled patronizingly as though this was a little below them after all. Then the conductor raised his wand—and, perhaps it was the champagne, for fifteen minutes I didn't stir in my chair.

I know so little about music that I can only make a story of it— which proves I've been told that it must have been low brow stuff. I don't mean that it had lonely music for the prehistoric ages with tiger-howls from the traps and a strain from "Onward Christian Soldiers" to mark the year 2 B. C. It wasn't like that. It started out with a weird, spinning sound, mostly from the cornets. Then there would be a series of interruptive notes which colored everything that came after them until before you knew it they became the theme and new discords were opposed outside. But just as you'd get used to the new discord one of the old themes would drop back in, this time as a discord, until you'd get a weird sense that it was a preposterous cycle after all. Long after the piece was over it went on and on in my head—whenever I think of that summer I can hear it yet.

It left me restless. Looking around I saw the figure of Gatsby standing alone on his steps looking from one group to another with watching eyes. I wondered if the fact that he was not drinking helped to set him off from his guests, for it seemed to me that he grew more and more alone as the fraternal hilarity increased. When the "Jazz History of the World" was over girls were putting their heads on men's shoulders in a puppyish, convivial way, girls were swooning backward playfully into men's arms, even into groups knowing that someone would arrest their falls—but no one swooned backward on Gatsby and no French bob touched Gatsby's shoulder and no singing quartets were formed with Gatsby's head for one link.

"Who is he anyhow?" I demanded of Jordan. "Who is Jay Gatsby? What does he do?"

"I haven't the faintest idea."

"But people don't just come out of nowhere and suddenly buy a palace on Long Island."

"Well, Gatsby did."

"But he must have some sort of a past. Tell me he comes from the lower east side or from Galena, Illinois, and I'll be satisfied——"

"I beg your pardon."

It was Gatsby's butler beside us.

"Miss Baker?" he inquired. "I beg your pardon but Mr. Gatsby is anxious to speak to you alone on an important matter."

"With *me?*" she exclaimed in surprise.

"Yes, madame."

She got up slowly, raising her eyebrows at me in astonishment, and followed the butler toward the house. I noticed that she wore her evening dress, all her dresses, like sports clothes—there was a jauntiness about her movements as if she had first learned to walk upon golf courses on clean, crisp mornings.

I was alone and it was almost two. For some time confused and intriguing sounds had issued from a long many-windowed room which overhung the terrace. Eluding Jordan's undergraduate who was now engaged in an obstetrical conversation with two chorus girls and who implored me to join him, I went inside.

The large room was full of people. One of the girls in yellow was playing the piano and beside her stood a tall red haired young lady from a famous chorus, engaged in song. She had drunk a quantity of champagne and during the course of her song she had decided ineptly that everything was very very sad—she was not only singing, she was weeping too. Whenever there was a pause in the song she filled it with gasping broken sobs and then took up the lyric again in a quavering soprano. The tears coursed down her cheeks—not freely, however, for when they came into contact with her heavily beaded eyelashes they assumed a deep inky color, and pursued the rest of their way in slow black rivulets. A humorous suggestion was made that she sing the notes on her face whereupon she threw up her hands, sank into a chair and went off into a deep vinous sleep.

"She had a fight with a man who says he's her husband," explained a girl at my elbow.

I looked around. Most of the remaining women were now having altercations with men said to be their husbands. Even Jordan's party, the quartet from East Egg, were rent asunder by dissension. One of the men was talking with curious intensity to a young actress, and his wife after attempting to laugh at the situation in a dignified and indifferent way broke down entirely and resorted to flank attacks—at intervals she appeared suddenly at his side like an angry diamond and hissed "You promised!" into his ear.

The reluctance to go home was not confined to wayward men. The hall was at present occupied by two deplorably sober men and their highly indignant wives. The wives were sympathizing with each other in slightly raised voices.

"Whenever he sees I'm having a good time he wants to go home."

"Never heard anything so selfish in my life."

"We're always the first ones to leave."

"So are we."

"Well, we're almost the last tonight," said one of the men sheepishly. "The orchestra left half an hour ago."

In spite of the wives' agreement that such malevolence was beyond credibility the dispute ended in a short struggle and both wives were lifted kicking out the door.

I was determined to wait until Jordan Baker emerged from her private interview with Gatsby. If he could inspire such sinister rumors I owed her that much protection for her courtesy of the evening. Once more I walked into the garden. Standing under the white plum tree were the movie director and the star, their faces touching except for a pale thin ray of moonlight between. It occurred to me that he had been very slowly bending toward her all evening to attain this proximity, and even while I watched I saw him stoop one ultimate degree and kiss at her cheek.

As I went in, Jordan Baker, just going out the front door, turned and waved good night. Gatsby was in the hall, bidding farewell to his last guests and bowing slightly over every woman's hand. I explained to him that I'd hunted for him early in the evening, and apologized for not having known him by name.

"Don't mention it," he enjoined me eagerly. "Don't give it another thought, old sport." The familiar expression held no more familiarity than the hand which reassuringly brushed my shoulder. "And don't forget we're going up in the hydroplane tomorrow morning at nine o'clock."

Then the butler behind his shoulder:

"Philadelphia wants you on the phone, sir."

"All right, in a minute. Tell them I'll be right there. . . . Good night."

"Good night."

"Good night. . . . Good night, old sport. . . . Good night."

But as I walked down the steps I saw that the evening was not quite over. Fifty feet from the door a dozen headlights illuminated a bizarre and tumultuous scene. In the ditch beside the road, right side up but violently shorn of one wheel, rested a new coupé which had left Gatsby's drive not two minutes before. The sharp jut of a wall accounted for the detachment of the wheel, which was now getting considerable attention from half a dozen curious chauffeurs. However, as they had left their cars blocking the road a harsh discordant din from those in the rear had been audible for some time and added to the already violent confusion of the scene.

A man in a long duster had dismounted from the wreck and now stood in the middle of the road looking from the car to the tire and from the tire to observers in a pleasant puzzled way.

"See!" he explained. "It went in the ditch."

The fact was infinitely astonishing to him—and I recognized first the amazing quality of wonder and then the man—it was the late patron of Gatsby's library.

"How'd it happen?"

He shrugged his shoulders.

"I know nothing whatever about mechanics," he said decisively.

"But how did it happen? Did you run into the wall?"

"Don't ask me," said Owl Eyes, washing his hands of the whole matter. "I know very little about driving—next to nothing at all. It happened, and that's all I know."

"Well, if you're a poor driver you oughtn't to try driving at night."

"But I wasn't even trying," he explained indignantly. "I wasn't even trying."

An awed hush fell upon the bystanders.

"Do you want to commit suicide?"

"You're lucky it was just a wheel! A bad driver and not even *try*ing!"

"You don't understand," explained the criminal. "I wasn't driving. There's another man in the car."

The shock that followed this declaration found voice in a sustained "Ah-h-h!" as the door of the coupé swung slowly open. The crowd—it was now a crowd—stepped back involuntarily and when the door had opened wide there was a ghostly pause. Then, very gradually, part by part, a pale dangling individual stepped out of the wreck, pawing tentatively at the ground with a large uncertain dancing shoe.

Blinded by the glare of the headlights and confused by the incessant groaning of the horns he stood swaying for a moment before he perceived the man in the duster.

"Wha's matter?" he inquired calmly. "Did we run outa gas?"

"Look!"

Half a dozen fingers pointed at the amputated wheel—he stared at it for a moment and then looked upward as though he suspected that it had dropped from the sky.

"It came off," someone explained.

He nodded.

"At first I din' notice we'd stopped."

A pause. Then taking a long breath and straightening his shoulders he remarked in a determined voice:

"Wonder'ff tell me where there's a gas'line station?"

At least a dozen men, some of them little better off than he was, explained to him that wheel and car were no longer joined by any physical bond.

"Back out," he suggested after a moment. "Put her in reverse."

"But the *wheel's off!*"

He hesitated.

"No harm in trying," he said.

The caterwauling horns had reached a crescendo and I turned away and cut across the lawn toward home. I glanced back once. A wafer of a moon was shining over Gatsby's house, making the night fine as before and surviving the laughter and the sound of his still glowing garden. A sudden emptiness seemed to flow now from the windows and the great doors, endowing with complete isolation the figure of the host, who stood on the porch, his hand up in a formal gesture of farewell.

Reading over what I have written so far I see I have given an impression that the events of three nights, several weeks apart, were all that absorbed me. On the contrary they were merely casual events in a crowded summer and they absorbed me infinitely less than my personal affairs.

Most of the time I worked. In the early morning the sun threw my shadow westward as I hurried down the white chasms of lower New York to the Probity Trust. I knew the other clerks and young bond-salesmen by their first names and lunched with them in dark crowded restaurants on little pig sausages and mashed potatoes and coffee. I even had a short affair with a girl who lived in Jersey City and worked in the accounting department but her brother began throwing mean looks in my direction so when she went on her vacation in July I let it blow quietly away.

I took dinner usually at the Yale Club—for some reason it was the gloomiest event of my day—and then I went upstairs to the library and studied investments and securities for a conscientious hour. There were generally a few rioters around but they never came into the library so it was a good place to work. After that if the night was mellow I strolled down Madison Avenue past the old Murray Hill Hotel and over 33d Street to the Pennsylvania Station.

I began to like New York, the racy adventurous feel of it at night and the satisfaction that the constant flicker of men and women and machines gives to the restless eye. I liked to walk up Fifth Avenue and pick out romantic women from the crowd and imagine that in a few minutes I was going to enter into their lives, and no one would ever know or disapprove. Sometimes, in my mind, I followed them to their apartments on the corners of hidden streets, and they turned and smiled back at me before they faded through a door into warm darkness. At the enchanted metropolitan twilight I felt a haunting loneliness sometimes, and felt it in others—poor young clerks who loitered in front of windows waiting until it was time for a solitary restaurant dinner—young clerks in the dusk, wasting the most poignant moments of night and life.

Again at eight o'clock, when the dark lanes of the Forties were lined five deep with throbbing taxi cabs, bound for the theatre district, when all New York turned about abruptly and pointed one way, I felt a sinking in my heart. Forms leaned together in the taxis as they waited, and voices sang, and there was laughter from unheard jokes, and lighted cigarettes made unintelligible circles inside. Imagining that I, too, was hurrying toward gayety and sharing their intimate excitement, I wished them well.

For a while I lost sight of Jordan Baker, and then in midsummer I found her again. At first I was flattered to go places with her because she was a golf champion and everyone knew her name. Then it was something more. I wasn't actually in love, but I felt a sort of tender curiosity. There was a reason behind her apparent contempt for things and people that interested me. When an attractive girl presents a bored, haughty face to the world, it frequently conceals an inconvenient responsiveness to love—but I knew it wasn't that. On the contrary, Jordan seemed to drift along in an arrested physical adolescence, and her greatest promise was to such men as me, who seek no love in a woman save what they have aroused deliberately and with difficulty themselves.

Yet Jordan's manner concealed something—all affectations conceal something eventually, even though they don't in the beginning—and eventually I found her out. When we were on a house party together up in Warwick, she left a borrowed car out in the rain with the top down, and then lied about it—and suddenly I remembered the story about her that had eluded me that night at Daisy's. At her first big golf tournament there had been a row that nearly reached the newspapers—a suggestion that she had moved her ball from a bad lie in the semi-final round. The thing had approached the proportions of a scandal—then died away. A caddy retracted his statement and the only other witness admitted that he might have been mistaken. The incident and the name had remained together in my mind.

Jordan Baker instinctively avoided clever shrewd men and now I saw that this was because she felt safer on a plane where any divergence from a code would be thought impossible. She was incurably dishonest. She wasn't able to endure being at a disadvantage, and given this unwillingness I suppose she had begun dealing in subterfuges when she was very young in order to keep that cool insolent smile turned to the world and yet satisfy the demands of her hard jaunty body.

It made no difference to me. Dishonesty in a woman is a thing you never blame deeply—I was casually sorry, and then I forgot. It was on that same house party that we had a curious conversation about driving a car. It started because she passed so close to some workmen that the fender flicked a button on one man's coat.

"You're a rotten driver," I protested. "Either you ought to be more careful or you oughtn't to drive at all."

"I am careful."

"No, you're not."

"Well, other people are," she said lightly.

"What's that got to do with it?"

"They'll keep out of my way," she insisted. "It takes two to make an accident."

"Suppose you met somebody just as careless as yourself."

"I hope I never will," she answered. "I hate careless people. That's why I like you."

Her grey, sun-strained eyes stared straight ahead but she had deliberately shifted our relations, and for a moment while the sunset was warm upon her face I thought I loved her. But I am slow thinking and full of interior rules that act as brakes on my desires, and I knew that first I had to get myself definitely out of that tangle back home. I'd been writing letters once a week and signing them "Love, Nick," and all I could think of was how, when she played tennis, a faint mustache of perspiration appeared on her upper lip.

Nevertheless there was a vague understanding that had to be tactfully broken off before I was free.

Everyone suspects himself of one of the cardinal virtues, and this is mine: I am one of the few honest people that I have ever known.

CHAPTER IV

On Sunday morning while church bells rang in the villages along shore, the world and its mistress returned to Gatsby's house and twinkled hilariously on his lawn.

"He's a bootlegger," said the young ladies, moving somewhere between his cocktails and his flowers. "One time he killed a man who had found out that he was nephew to von Hindenburg and second cousin to the devil. Reach me a rose, honey, and pour me a last drop into that there crystal glass."

Once I wrote down on the empty spaces of a time-table the names of those who came to Gatsby's house that summer. It is an old time-table now, degenerating at its folds and headed "This schedule in effect July 5th, 1921." But I can still read the grey names and they will give you a better impression than my generalities of those who accepted Gatsby's hospitality and paid him the subtle tribute of knowing nothing whatever about him.

From West Egg, then, came the Chester Beckers and the Leeches and a man named Bunsen whom I knew at Yale and Doctor Webster Civet who was drowned last summer up in Maine. And the Hornbeams and the Willie Voltaires and a whole clan named Blackbuck who always gathered in a corner and flipped up their noses like goats at whosoever came near. And the Ismays and the Chrysties (or rather Hubert Auerbach and Mr. Chrystie's wife) and Edgar Beaver whose hair they say turned cotton-white one winter afternoon for no good reason at all.

Clarence Endive was from West Egg, as I remember. He came only once, in white knickerbockers, and had a fight with a tough named Etty in the garden. From farther out on the Island came the Cheadles and the O. R. P. Schraeders and the Stonewall Jackson Abrams of Georgia, still violently impassioned about the Civil War, and the Fishguards and the Ripley Snells. Snell was there three days before he went to the penitentiary, so drunk out on the gravel

drive that Mrs. Ulysses Swett's automobile ran over his right hand.
The Dancies came too and S. B. Whitebait, who was well over
sixty, and Maurice A. Flink and the Hammerheads and Beluga the
tobacco importer and Beluga's girls.

From East Egg came the Poles and the Mulreadys and Cecil
Roebuck and Cecil Schoen and Gulick, the state senator, and
Newton Orchid who controlled Films Par Excellence and Eckhaust
and Clyde Cohen and Don S. Schwartze (the son) and Arthur
McCarty, all connected with the movies in one way or another.
And the Catlips and Bembergs and G. Earl Muldoon, brother to
that Muldoon who afterwards strangled his wife. Da Fontano the
promoter came there and Ed Legros and James B. ("Rot-Gut")
Ferret and the de Jongs and Ernest Lilly—they came to gamble and
when Ferret wandered into the garden it meant he was cleaned out
and Associated Traction would have to fluctuate profitably next
day.

A man named Klipspringer was there so often and so long that
he became known as "the boarder"—I doubt if he had any other
home. Of theatrical people there were Gus Waize and Horace
O'Donavan and Lester Myer and George Duckweed and Francis
Bull. Also from New York were the Chromes and the Backhyssons
and the Dennickers and Russel Betty and the Corrigans and the
Kellehers and the Dewars and the Scullys and S. W. Belcher and the
Smirkes and the young Quinns, divorced now, and Henry L.
Palmetto who killed himself by jumping in front of a subway train
in Times Square.

Benny McClenahan arrived always with four girls. They were
never quite the same ones in physical person but they were so
identical with one another that it inevitably seemed they had been
there before. I have forgotten their names—Jaqueline, I think, or
else Consuela or Gloria or Judy or June, and their last names were
either the melodious names of flowers and months or the sterner
ones of the great American capitalists whose cousins, if pressed,
they would confess themselves to be.

In addition to all these I can remember that the Ascott-Joneses
came there at least once and the Cockerell girls and young Brewer
who had his nose shot off in the war and Mr. Albrucksburger and

Miss Haag, his fiancée, and Ardita Fitz-Peters and Mr. P. Jewett, once head of the American Legion, and Miss Claudia Hip with a man reputed to be her chauffeur, and a prince of something whom we called Duke and whose name, if I ever knew it, I have forgotten.

All these people came to Gatsby's house in the summer.

At nine o'clock one morning late in July Gatsby's gorgeous car lurched up the rocky drive to my door and gave out a burst of melody from its three noted horn. It was the first time he had called on me though I had gone to two of his parties, mounted in his hydroplane, and, at his polite invitation, made frequent use of his beach.

"Hello, old sport," he said. "You're having lunch with me in the city today and I thought you might like to ride up now."

That formal caution that enveloped his every word was less perceptible in the daytime; as he stood balancing on the running board of his car he seemed very natural, after all. His body had about it that American resourcefulness of movement—a characteristic that is due, I suppose, to the absence of heavy lifting work in youth and, even more, to the formless grace of our nervous sporadic games.

"I suppose you've seen my car?"

I'd seen it. Everybody had seen it. It was a rich cream color, bright with nickel, swollen here and there in its monstrous length with triumphant hatboxes and supper-boxes and tool-boxes, and terraced with a labyrinth of wind-shields that mirrored a dozen suns.

"Handsomest car in New York," he informed me. "I know it's pretty gay, but what's the use of riding around in a big hearse?"

Sitting down behind many layers of glass in a sort of green leather conservatory we started to town.

"I've got a favor to ask you, old sport," he said, "and I want to inquire one thing before I begin."

"All right."

"Have you ever had what's known as an affaire de coeur?"

"Why—never a very serious one."

"Never?" he insisted.

"Never."

He patted the knee of his caramel-colored suit.

"Very well," he decided. "I'll have to begin in a different way. Let me ask you this: What's your opinion of me anyhow?"

A little overwhelmed I began the generalized evasions which that question deserves.

"Be frank, old sport," he urged me.

But I didn't know what I thought of him yet, and so as a facetious substitute I passed on to him, as well as I could remember, the various sinister accusations that had flavored conversation in his halls.

"I'll tell you God's truth." His right hand suddenly ordered divine retribution to stand by. "I am the son of some wealthy people in the middle-west—all dead now. I was brought up in America but educated at Oxford because all my ancestors have been educated there for many years. It's a sort of tradition."

He looked at me sideways—and I know why Jordan Baker had believed he was lying. He hurried the phrase "educated at Oxford," or swallowed it or choked on it as though it had bothered him before. And with this doubt his whole statement fell to pieces and I wondered if there wasn't something a little sinister about him after all.

"What part of the middle-west?" I inquired casually.

"San Francisco."

"I see."

"My family all died and I came into a good deal of money."

His voice was solemn as if the memory of that sudden extinction of a clan still haunted him. For a moment I suspected that he was pulling my leg but a glance at him convinced me otherwise.

"After that I lived like a young rajah in all the capitals of Europe—Paris, Vienna, Rome—collecting jewels, chiefly rubies, hunting big game, painting a little, things for myself only and trying to forget something very sad that had happened to me long ago."

With an effort I managed to restrain my incredulous laughter. The very phrases were worn so threadbare that they evoked no image except that of a turbanned "character" leaking sawdust at every pore as he pursued a tiger through the Bois de Boulogne.

"Then came the war, old sport. It was a great relief and I tried very hard to die but I seemed to bear an enchanted life. I accepted a commission as second lieutenant when it began. In the Argonne Forest I took the remains of my machine-gun battalion so far forward that there was a half mile gap on either side of us where the infantry couldn't advance. We stayed there two days and two nights, a hundred and ninety men with fourteen Lewis guns, and when the infantry came up at last they found the insignia of three German divisions among the piles of dead. I was promoted to be a major and every Allied government gave me a decoration—even Montenegro, little Montenegro down on the Adriatic Sea!"

Little Montenegro! He lifted up the words and nodded at them with a faint smile. My incredulity had turned to fascination now; it was like skimming hastily through a dozen magazines.

He reached in his pocket and a piece of metal, slung on a ribbon, fell into my palm.

"That's the one from Montenegro."

To my astonishment the thing had an authentic look. "*Orderi di Danilo,*" ran the circular legend, "*Montenegro, Nicolas Rex.*"

"Turn it."

"*Major Jay Gatsby,*" I read, "*For Valour Extraordinary.*"

"Here's another thing I always carry. A souvenir of Oxford days. It was taken in Trinity Quad—the man on my left is now the Earl of Doncaster."

It was a photograph of half a dozen young men in blazers loafing in front of an archway through which were visible a host of spires. There was Gatsby, looking a little, not much, younger—with a cricket bat in his hand.

Then it was all true. I saw the skins of tigers flaming in his palace on the Grand Canal; I saw him opening a chest of rubies to ease, with their crimson-lighted depths, the gnawings of his broken heart; I saw his family fading away in their palatial home in San Francisco and leaving their fortune to a reckless young major at the wars.

"I'm going to make a great request of you today," he said,

pocketing his souvenirs, "so I thought you ought to know something about me. I didn't want you to think I was just a—just a nobody."

I'd never thought that. Now I began to believe that he was an extraordinary idealist, and fatuous only as all men are who have actually achieved their own ideals.

"I usually find myself among strangers because I drift here and there trying to forget the sad thing that happened to me." He hesitated, "but I came here to remember, not to forget. You'll hear about it this afternoon."

"At lunch?"

"No, this afternoon. I happened to find out that you're taking Miss Baker to tea."

"Do you mean you're in love with Miss Baker?"

"No, old sport, I'm not. But she's kindly consented to tell you the story."

This annoyed me. I hadn't asked Jordan to tea in order to discuss Jay Gatsby. The man had his nerve, and for a moment I was sorry I'd ever set foot on his overpopulated lawn.

"But what business is it of mine, Mr. Gatsby?"

He wouldn't say another word. His dignity or his aloofness grew on him as we neared the city. We passed Port Roosevelt, where there was a glimpse of red-belted ocean-going ships, and sped along a cobbled slum lined with the dark, undeserted saloons of the faded gilt nineteen-hundreds. Then the valley of ashes opened out on all sides of us, and I had a glimpse of Mrs. Wilson straining at the garage pump with panting vitality as we went by.

With fenders spread like wings we scattered light through half Astoria—only half, for as we twisted among the pillars of the elevated I heard the familiar "jug-jug-*spat!*" of a motorcycle, and a frantic policeman rode alongside.

"All right, old sport," called Gatsby. We slowed down; taking a white card from his wallet he waved it before the policeman's eyes.

"Right you are," agreed the policeman, tipping his cap. "Know you next time, Mr. Gatsby. Excuse *me!*"

"What was that?" I inquired. "The picture of Oxford?"

"I did the commissioner a favor once, and he sends me a Christmas card once a year."

Over the great bridge, with the sunlight through the girders making a constant flicker upon the moving cars, with the city rising up across the river in white heaps and sugar lumps all built with a wish out of non-olfactory money. The city seen from the Queensboro Bridge is always the city seen for the first time, in its first wild promise of all the mystery and the beauty in the world.

A dead man passed us in a hearse heaped with blooms, followed by two carriages with drawn blinds and by more cheerful carriages for friends. The friends looked out at us with the tragic eyes and short upper lips of south-eastern Europe and I was glad that the sight of Gatsby's splendid car was included in their somber holiday. As we crossed Blackwells Island a limousine passed us, driven by a white chauffeur, in which sat three modish negroes, two bucks and a girl. I laughed aloud as the yolks of their eyeballs rolled toward us in haughty rivalry.

"Anything can happen now that we've rolled over this bridge," I thought; "anything at all. . . ."

Even Gatsby could happen, without any particular wonder.

Roaring noon. In a well-fanned Forty-second Street cellar I met Gatsby for lunch. Blinking away the brightness of the street outside my eyes picked him out obscurely in the ante-room, talking to another man.

"Mr. Carraway, this is my friend Mr. Wolfshiem."

A small flat-nosed Jew raised his large head and regarded me with two fine growths of hair which luxuriated in either nostril. After a moment I discovered his tiny eyes in the half darkness.

"—so I took one look at him—" said Mr. Wolfshiem, shaking my hand earnestly, "—and what do you think I did?"

"What?" I inquired politely.

But evidently he was not addressing me for he dropped my hand and covered Gatsby with his expressive nose.

"I handed the money to Mark and I sid, 'All right, Mark, don't pay him a penny till he shuts his mouth.' He shut it then and there."

Gatsby took an arm of each of us and moved forward into the restaurant whereupon Mr. Wolfshiem swallowed a new sentence he was starting and lapsed into a somnambulatory abstraction.

"Highballs?" asked the headwaiter.

"This is a nice restaurant here," said Mr. Wolfshiem looking at the contented nymphs on the ceiling. "But I like across the street better!"

"Yes, highballs," agreed Gatsby, and then to Mr. Wolfshiem: "It's too hot over there."

"Hot and small—yes," said Mr. Wolfshiem, "but full of memories."

"What place is that?" I asked.

"The old Metropole."

"The old Metropole," said Mr. Wolfshiem gloomily. "Filled with faces dead and gone. Filled with friends gone now forever. I can't forget so long as I live the night they shot Rosy Rosenthal there. It was six of us at the table and Rosy had eat and drunk a lot all evening. When it was almost morning the waiter came up to him with a funny look and says somebody wants to speak to him outside. 'All right' says Rosy and begins to get up and I pulled him down in his chair.

"'Let the bastards come in here if they want you, Rosy, but don't you, so help me, move outside this room.'

"It was four o'clock in the morning then and if we'd of raised the blinds we'd of seen daylight."

"Did he go?" I asked innocently.

"Sure he went"—Mr. Wolfshiem's nose flashed at me indignantly. "He turned around in the door and says, 'Don't let that waiter take away my coffee!' Then he went out on the sidewalk and they shot him three times in his full belly and drove away."

"Four of them were electrocuted," I said, remembering.

"Five with Becker." His nostrils turned to me in an interested way. "I understand you're looking for a business gonnegtion."

The juxtaposition of these two remarks was startling. Gatsby answered for me.

"Oh, no," he exclaimed, "this isn't the man."

"No?" Mr. Wolfshiem seemed disappointed.

"This is just a friend. I told you we'd talk about that some other time."

"I beg your pardon," said Mr. Wolfshiem. "I had a wrong man."

A succulent hash arrived and Mr. Wolfshiem, forgetting the more sentimental atmosphere of the old Metropole, began to eat with ferocious delicacy. His eyes, meanwhile, roved very slowly all around the room—he completed the arc by turning to inspect the people directly behind. I think that, except for my presence, he would have taken one short glance beneath our own table.

"Look here, old sport," said Gatsby leaning toward me. "I'm afraid I made you a little angry this morning in the car."

"Not at all, Mr. Gatsby. Though I don't understand why your request has to come through Miss Baker."

"You will this afternoon. You'll find it's a very natural situation after all. She's a fine sportswoman and she'd never do anything even faintly questionable."

Suddenly Gatsby looked at his watch, jumped up and hurried from the room leaving me with Mr. Wolfshiem at the table.

"He has to telephone," said Mr. Wolfshiem, following him with his eyes. "Fine fellow, isn't he? Handsome to look at and a perfect gentleman."

"Yes."

"He's an Oggsford man."

"Oh."

"He went to Oggsford College in England. You know Oggsford College?"

"I've heard of it."

"It's one of the most famous colleges in the world."

"Have you known Gatsby for a long time?" I inquired.

"Several years," he answered in a gratified way. "I made the pleasure of his acquaintance just after the war. But I knew I had discovered a man of fine breeding after I talked with him an hour. I said to myself, there's the kind of man you'd like to take home and introduce to your mother and sister." He paused. "I see you're looking at my cuff buttons."

I hadn't been looking at them, but I did now. They were composed of irregular pieces of ivory.

"Finest specimens of human molars," he informed me.

"Well!" I inspected them. "That's a very interesting idea."

"Yeah." He flipped his sleeves up under his coat. "Yeah, Gatsby's very careful about women. He would never so much as look at a friend's wife."

When the subject of this instinctive trust returned to the table and sat down Mr. Wolfshiem drank his coffee with a jerk and got to his feet.

"I have enjoyed my lunch," he said, "and I'm going to run off from you two young men before I outstay my welcome."

"Don't hurry, Meyer," said Gatsby, without enthusiasm. Mr. Wolfshiem raised his hand in a sort of benediction.

"You're very polite but I belong to another generation," he announced solemnly. "You sit here and discuss your sports and your young ladies and your——" He supplied an imaginary noun with another wave of his hand—— "As for me I am fifty years old, and I won't impose myself on you any longer."

As he shook hands and turned away his tragic nose was trembling. I wondered if I had said anything to offend him.

"He becomes very sentimental sometimes," explained Gatsby. "This is one of his sentimental days. He's quite a character around New York—a denizen of Broadway."

"Who is he anyhow—an actor?"

"No."

"A dentist?"

"Meyer Wolfshiem? No, he's a gambler." Gatsby hesitated, then added coolly: "He's the man who fixed the World's Series back in 1919."

"Fixed the World's Series?" I repeated.

The idea staggered me. I knew of course that the World's Series had been fixed in 1919 but if I had thought of it at all I would have thought of it as a thing that merely *happened*, the end of some inevitable chain. It never occurred to me that one man could start to play with the faith of fifty million people—with the single-mindedness of a burglar blowing a safe.

"How did he happen to do that?" I asked after a minute.

"He just saw the opportunity."

"Why isn't he in jail?"

"They can't get him, old sport. He's a smart man."

I insisted on paying the check; as the waiter brought my change I caught sight of Tom Buchanan on the other side of the crowded room.

"Come along with me for a minute," I said. "I've got to say hello to a man."

When we came near Tom jumped up and took half a dozen steps in our direction.

"Where've you been?" he demanded eagerly. "Daisy's furious because you haven't called up."

"This is Mr. Gatsby, Mr. Buchanan."

They shook hands briefly and a strained, unfamiliar look of embarrassment came over Gatsby's face.

Tom turned to me:

"How've you been, anyhow? How'd you happen to come up this far to eat?"

"I've been having lunch with Mr. Gatsby——"

I turned toward Mr. Gatsby, but he was no longer there.

One October day in nineteen-seventeen—(said Jordan Baker that afternoon, sitting up very straight on a straight chair in the tea-room of the Plaza Hotel)—I was walking along from one place to another half on the sidewalks and half on the lawns. I was more satisfied on the lawns because I had on shoes from England with rubber nobs on the soles that bit into the soft ground. I had on a new plaid skirt also that blew a little in the wind and whenever this happened the red, white and blue banners in front of all the houses stretched out stiff and said *tut-tut-tut-tut* in a disapproving way.

The largest of the banners and the largest of the lawns belonged to Daisy Fay's house. She was just eighteen, two years older than me, and by far the most popular of all the young girls in Louisville. She dressed in white and had a little white car and all day long the telephone rang in her house and excited young officers from Camp Taylor demanded the privilege of monopolizing her that night, "anyways for an hour!"

When I came opposite her house that morning her white car was beside the curb, and she was sitting in it with a lieutenant I had never seen before. They were so engrossed in each other that she didn't see me until I was five feet away.

"Hello Jordan," she called unexpectedly. "Please come here."

I was flattered that she wanted to speak to me because of all the older girls I admired her most. She asked me if I was going to the Red Cross and make bandages. I was. Well, then, would I tell Mrs. Tom Partridge that she couldn't come that day? The officer looked at her while Daisy was speaking, in a way that every young girl wants to be looked at sometime, and because it seemed romantic to me I have remembered the incident ever since. His name was Jay Gatsby and I didn't lay eyes on him again for almost five years— even after I'd met him on Long Island I didn't realize it was the same man.

That was nineteen-seventeen. By the next year I had a few beaux myself, and I began to play in tournaments, so I didn't see Daisy very often. She went with a slightly older crowd—when she went with anyone at all. Rather wild rumors were circulating about her—how her mother had found her packing her bag one winter night to go to New York and say goodbye to a soldier who was going overseas. She was effectually prevented, but she wasn't on speaking terms with her family for several weeks. After that she didn't play around with the soldiers any more but only with a few flat-footed, short-sighted young men in town who couldn't get into the army at all.

By the next autumn she was gay again, gay as ever. She had a debut after the armistice, and in February she was presumably engaged to a man from New Orleans. In June she married Tom Buchanan of Chicago with more pomp and circumstance than Louisville ever knew before. He came down from Chicago with a hundred people in four private cars and hired a floor of the Mulbach Hotel, and the day before the wedding he gave her a string of pearls valued at seven hundred and fifty thousand dollars.

I was a bridesmaid. I came into her room half an hour before the bridal dinner and found her lying on her bed as lovely as the June night in her flowered dress—and as drunk as a monkey. She had a bottle of sauterne in one hand and a letter in the other.

"'Gratulate me," she muttered. "Never had a drink before but oh, how I do enjoy it."

"What's the matter, Daisy?"

I was scared, I can tell you. I'd never seen a girl like that before.

"Here, dearis." She groped around in a waste-basket she had with her on the bed and pulled out the string of pearls. "Take 'em downstairs and give 'em back to whoever they belong to. Tell 'em all Daisy's change' her min'. Say 'Daisy's change' her min'!"

She began to cry—she cried and cried. I rushed out and found her mother's maid and we locked the door and got her into a cold bath. She wouldn't let go of the letter. She took it into the tub with her and squeezed it up into a wet ball and only let me leave it in the soap dish when she saw that it was coming to pieces like snow.

But she didn't say another word. We gave her spirits of ammonia and put ice on her forehead and hooked her back into her dress and half an hour later when we walked out of the room the pearls were around her neck and the outbreak was over. Next day at five o'clock she married Tom Buchanan without so much as a shiver and started off on a three months' trip to the South Seas.

I saw them in Santa Barbara when they came back and I thought I'd never seen a girl so mad about her husband. If he left the room for a minute she'd look around uneasily and say "Where's Tom gone?" and wear the most abstracted expression until she saw him coming in the door. She used to sit on the sand with his head in her lap by the hour rubbing her fingers over his eyes and looking at him with unfathomable delight. It was touching to see them together—it made you laugh in a hushed, fascinated way. That was in August. A week after I left Santa Barbara Tom ran into a wagon on the Ventura road one night and ripped a front wheel off his car. The girl who was with him got into the papers too because she broke her arm—she was one of the chambermaids in the Santa Barbara Hotel.

The next April Daisy had her little girl and they went to France for a year. I saw them one spring in Cannes and later in Deauville and then they came back to Chicago to settle down. Daisy was popular in Chicago, as you know. They moved with a fast crowd, all of them young and rich and wild, but she came out with an absolutely perfect reputation. Perhaps because she doesn't drink. It's a great advantage not to drink among hard drinking people. You can hold your tongue and, moreover, you can time any little irregularity of your own so that everybody else is so blind that they don't see or care. Perhaps Daisy never went in for amour at all—and yet there's something in that voice of hers. . . .

Well, about a month ago, she heard the name Gatsby for the first time in years. It was when I asked you—do you remember?—if you knew Gatsby in West Egg. After you had gone home she came into my room and woke me up and asked me "What Gatsby?" and when I described him—I was half asleep—she said in the strangest voice that it must be the man she used to know. It wasn't until then that I connected this Gatsby with the officer in her white car.

When Jordan Baker had finished telling me this we had left the Plaza for half an hour and were driving in a Victoria through Central Park. The sun had gone down behind the tall apartments of the movie stars in the West Fifties and the clear voices of children, already gathered like crickets on the grass, rose through the hot twilight:

> *"I'm the Sheik of Araby*
> *Your love belongs to me*
> *At night when you're asleep*
> *Into your tent I'll creep——"*

"It was a strange coincidence," I said.

"But it wasn't a coincidence at all."

"Why not?"

"Gatsby bought that house so that Daisy would be just across the bay."

Then it had not been merely the stars to which he had aspired on that June night. He came alive to me, delivered suddenly from the womb of his purposeless splendor.

"He wants to know—" continued Jordan "—if you'll invite Daisy to your house some afternoon and then let him come over."

The modesty of the demand shook me. He had waited five years and bought a mansion where he dispensed starlight to casual moths—so that he could "come over" some afternoon to a stranger's garden.

"Did I have to know all this before he could ask such a little thing?"

"He's afraid. He's waited so long. He thought you might be offended. You see he's a regular tough underneath it all."

Something worried me.

"Why didn't he ask you to arrange a meeting?"

"He wants her to see his house," she explained. "And your house is right next door."

"Oh!"

"I think he half expected her to wander into one of his parties, some night," went on Jordan, "but she never did. Then he began asking people casually if they knew her, and I was the first one he found. It was that night he sent for me at his dance, and you should have heard the elaborate way he worked up to it. Of course, I immediately suggested a luncheon in New York—and I thought he'd go mad.

"'I don't want to do anything out of the way!' he kept saying. 'I want to see her right next door.'

"When I said you were a particular friend of Tom's he wanted to abandon the whole idea. He doesn't know anything about Tom, though he says he's read a Chicago paper for years just on the chance of catching a glimpse of her name."

It was dark now and as we dipped under a little bridge I put my arm around Jordan and drew her toward me and asked her to dinner. Suddenly I wasn't thinking of Daisy and Gatsby any more, but of this clean, hard, limited person who dealt in universal skepticism and who leaned back jauntily just within the circle of my arm. A phrase began to beat in my ears with a sort of heady excitement: "There are only the pursued, the pursuing, the busy and the tired."

"And Daisy ought to have something in her life," murmured Jordan to me.

"Does she want to see Gatsby?"

"She's not to know about it. Gatsby doesn't want her to know. You're just supposed to invite her to tea."

We passed a barrier of dark trees and then the façade of Fifty-ninth Street, a block of delicate pale light, beamed down into the

Park. Unlike Gatsby and Tom Buchanan I had no girl whose disembodied face floated along the dark cornices and blinding signs and so I drew up the girl beside me, tightening my arms. Her wan scornful mouth smiled and so I drew her up again, closer, this time to my face.

CHAPTER V

When I came home to West Egg that night I was afraid for a moment that my house was on fire. Two o'clock and the whole corner of the peninsula was blazing with light which fell unreal on the shrubbery and made thin elongating glints upon the roadside wires. Turning a corner I saw that it was Gatsby's house, lit from tower to cellar.

At first I thought it was another party, a wild rout that had resolved itself into "hide-and-seek" or "sardines-in-the-box" with all the house thrown open to the game. But there wasn't a sound. Only wind in the trees which blew the wires and made the lights go off and on again as if the house had winked into the darkness. As my taxi groaned away I saw Gatsby walking toward me across his lawn.

"Your place looks like the world's fair," I said.

"Does it?" He glanced back at it absently. "I've been looking into some of the rooms. Let's go to Coney Island, old sport. In my car."

"I've got to go to bed."

"All right."

He waited, looking at me with suppressed eagerness.

"I talked with Miss Baker," I said after a moment. "I'm going to call up Daisy tomorrow and invite her over here to tea."

"Oh, that's all right," he said carelessly. "I don't want to put you to any trouble."

"What day would suit you?"

"What day would suit *you*?" he corrected me quickly. "I don't want to put you to any trouble, you know."

"How about the day after tomorrow?"

He considered for a moment. Then, with reluctance:

"I want to get the grass cut," he said.

We both looked down at the grass—there was a sharp line where my ragged lawn ended and the darker, well-kept expanse of his began. I suspected that he meant my grass.

I was light-headed and happy that night; I think I walked into a deep sleep as I entered my front door. So I don't know whether or not he went to Coney Island or for how many hours he "looked into rooms" while his house blazed gaudily on. I called up Daisy from the office next morning and invited her to come to tea.

"Don't bring Tom," I said.

"What?"

"Don't bring Tom."

"Who is 'Tom'?" she asked innocently.

The day agreed upon was pouring rain. At eleven a man in a raincoat dragging a lawn-mower tapped at my front door and said that Mr. Gatsby had sent him over to cut my grass. This reminded me that I had forgotten to tell my Finn to come back and make tea so I drove into West Egg to search for her among soggy white-washed alleys and to buy some cups and lemons and flowers.

The flowers were unnecessary, for at two o'clock a greenhouse arrived from Gatsby's, with innumerable receptacles to hold the bunches. At three the front door opened nervously and Gatsby in a white flannel suit, silver shirt and gold colored tie hurried in. He was pale and there were dark signs of sleeplessness beneath his eyes.

"Is everything all right?" he asked immediately.

"The grass looks fine, if that's what you mean."

"What grass?" he inquired blankly. "Oh, the grass in the yard." He looked out the window at it, but judging from his expression I don't believe he saw a thing.

"Looks very good," he remarked vaguely. "One of the papers said they thought the rain would stop about four. I think it was "The Times." Have you got everything you need in the shape of— of tea?"

I took him into the pantry where he looked a little reproachfully at the Finn. Together we scrutinized the twelve lemon cakes from the delicatessen shop.

"Will they do?" I asked.

"Of course, of course! They're fine!" and he added hollowly, ". . . old sport."

The rain cooled about half past three to a damp mist through which occasional thin drops swam like dew. Gatsby looked with vacant eyes through a copy of Clay's "Economics," starting at the Finnish woman's tread as it shook the kitchen floor and peering toward the bleared windows from time to time as if a series of invisible but alarming incidents were taking place outside. Finally he got up and informed me in an uncertain voice that he was going home.

"Why's that?"

"Nobody's coming to tea. It's too late!" He looked at his watch as if there was some pressing demand on his time elsewhere. "I can't wait all day."

"Don't be silly; it's just two minutes to four."

He sat down, miserably, as if I had pushed him, and simultaneously there was the sound of a motor turning into my lane. We both jumped up and, a little harrowed myself, I went out into the yard.

Under the dripping bare lilac trees a large open car was coming up the drive. It stopped. Daisy's face, tipped sideways beneath a three-cornered lavender hat, looked out at me with a bright ecstatic smile.

"Is this absolutely where you live, my dearest one?"

The exhilarating ripple of her voice was like a wild tonic in the rain. I had to follow the sound of it for a moment, up and down, with my ear alone before any words came through. A damp streak of hair lay like a dash of blue paint across her cheek and her hand was wet with glistening drops as I took it to help her from the car.

"Are you in love with me?" she said low in my ear. "Or why did I have to come alone?"

"That's the secret of Castle Rackrent. Tell your chauffeur to go far away and spend an hour."

"Come back in an hour, Ferdie." Then in a grave murmur, "His name is Ferdie."

"Does the gasoline affect his nose?"

"I don't think so," she said innocently. "Why?"

We went in. To my overwhelming surprise the living room was deserted.

"Well, that's funny!" I exclaimed.

"What's funny?"

She turned her head as there was a light, dignified knocking at the front door. I went out and opened it. Gatsby, pale as death, with his hands plunged like weights in his coat pockets, was standing in a puddle of water glaring tragically into my eyes.

With his hands still in his coat pockets he stalked by me into the hall, turned sharply as if he were on a wire, and disappeared into the living room. It wasn't a bit funny. Aware of the loud beating of my own heart I pulled the door to against the increasing rain.

For half a minute there wasn't a sound. Then from the living room I heard a sort of choking murmur and part of a laugh followed by Daisy's voice on a clear artificial note.

"I certainly am awfully glad to see you again."

A pause; it endured horribly. I had nothing to do in the hall so I went into the room.

Gatsby, his hands still in his pockets, was reclining against the mantelpiece in a strained counterfeit of perfect ease, even of boredom. His head leaned back so far that it rested against the face of a defunct mantelpiece clock and from this position his distraught eyes stared down at Daisy who was sitting frightened but graceful on the edge of a stiff chair.

"We've met before," muttered Gatsby. His eyes glanced momentarily at me and his lips parted as though with some abortive attempt at a laugh. Luckily the clock took this moment to tilt dangerously at the pressure of his head, whereupon he turned and caught it with trembling fingers and set it back in place. Then he sat down, rigidly, his elbow on the arm of the sofa and his chin in his hand.

"I'm sorry about the clock," he said.

My own face had now assumed a deep tropical burn. I couldn't muster up a single commonplace out of the thousand in my head.

"It's an old clock," I told them idiotically.

I think we all believed for a moment that it had smashed in pieces on the floor.

"We haven't met in over three years," said Daisy, her voice as matter of fact as it could ever be.

"Five years next November."

The automatic quality of Gatsby's answer set us all back at least another minute. I had them both on their feet with the desperate suggestion that they help me make tea in the kitchen when the demoniac Finn brought it in on a tray.

Amid the welcome confusion of cups and cakes a certain physical decency established itself. Gatsby got himself into a shadow and while Daisy and I talked looked conscientiously from one to the other of us with tense unhappy eyes. However, as calmness wasn't an end in itself I made an excuse at the first possible moment and got to my feet.

"Where are you going?" demanded Gatsby in immediate alarm.

"I'll be back."

"I've got to speak to you about something before you go."

He followed me wildly into the kitchen, closed the door and whispered "Oh, God!" in a miserable way.

"What's the matter?"

"This is a terrible mistake," he said, shaking his head from side to side, "a terrible, terrible mistake."

"You're just embarrassed, that's all," and luckily I added: "Daisy's embarrassed too."

"She's embarrassed?" he repeated incredulously.

"Just as much as you are."

"Don't talk so loud."

"You're acting like a little boy," I broke out impatiently. "Not only that but you're rude. Daisy's sitting in there all alone."

He raised his hand to stop my words, looked at me with unforgettable reproach and opening the door cautiously went back into the other room.

I walked out the back way, just as Gatsby had when he had made his nervous circuit of the house half an hour before, and ran for a huge black knotted tree, whose massed leaves made a fabric against the rain. Once more it was pouring, and my irregular lawn, well-shaved by Gatsby's gardener, abounded in small muddy swamps and prehistoric marshes. There was nothing to look at from under the tree except Gatsby's enormous house so I stared at it, like Kant at his church steeple, for half an hour. A brewer had built it early in the "period" craze, a decade before, and there was a story that he'd agreed to pay five years' tax on all the neighboring cottages if their owners would have the roofs thatched with straw. Perhaps their refusal took the heart out of his plan to Found a Family—he went into an immediate decline. His children sold his house with the black wreath still on the door. Americans, while willing, even eager, to be serfs, have always been obstinate about being peasantry.

After half an hour the sun shone again and the grocer's automobile rounded Gatsby's drive with the raw material for his servants' dinner—I felt sure he wouldn't eat a spoonful. A maid began opening the upper windows of his house, appeared momentarily in each and, pausing in the large central bay, leaned out and spat meditatively into the garden. It was time I went back. While the rain continued it had seemed like the murmur of their voices, rising and swelling a little, now and then, with gusts of emotion. But in the new silence I felt that silence had fallen within the house too.

I went in—after making every possible noise in the kitchen short of pushing over the stove—but I don't believe they heard a sound. They were sitting at either end of the couch looking at each other as if some question had been asked or was in the air, and every vestige of embarrassment was gone. Daisy's face was smeared with tears and when I came in she jumped up and began wiping at it with her handkerchief before a mirror. But there was a change in Gatsby that was simply confounding. He literally glowed; without a word or a gesture of exultation a new well-being radiated from him and filled the little room.

"Oh, hello, old sport," he said, as if he hadn't seen me for years. I thought for a moment he was going to shake hands.

"It's stopped raining."

"Has it?" When he realized what I was talking about, that there were twinkle-bells of sunshine in the room, he became overjoyed, and repeated it to Daisy. "What do you think of that? It's stopped raining."

"I'm glad, Jay." Her throat, full of aching, grieving beauty, told only of her unexpected joy.

"I want you and Daisy to come over to my house," he said. "I'd like to show her around."

"You're sure you want me to come?"

"Absolutely, old sport."

Daisy went upstairs to wash her face—too late I thought with humiliation of my towels—while Gatsby and I waited on the lawn. "My house looks well, doesn't it?" he demanded. "See how the whole front of it catches the light."

"It's awfully nice."

"Yes." His eyes went over it, every arched door and square tower. "In three years I earned that."

"I thought you inherited your money."

"But I lost most of it in the big panic, old sport—the panic of the war."

Daisy came out of the house and the two rows of brass buttons on her dress gleamed in the sunlight.

"That huge place *there?*" she cried pointing.

"Do you like it?"

"I love it, but I don't see how you live there all alone."

"I keep it always full of interesting people, night and day. People who do interesting things. Celebrated people."

Instead of taking the short cut along the Sound we went down to the road and entered by the big postern. With enchanting murmurs Daisy admired this aspect or that of the feudal silhouette against the sky, admired the gardens, the sparkling odor of the jonquils, and the frothy odor of hawthorn and plum blossoms, and the pale gold odor of kiss-me-by-the-gate. It was strange to reach the marble steps and find no stir of bright dresses in and out the door and hear no sound but bird voices in the trees.

And inside as we wandered through Marie Antoinette music rooms and Restoration salons I felt that there were guests concealed behind every couch and table, under orders to be breathlessly silent until we had passed through. As Gatsby closed the door of "the Merton College Library" I could have sworn I heard the owl-eyed man break into ghostly laughter.

We went upstairs, through period bedrooms swathed in rose and lavender silk and vivid with new flowers, through dressing rooms and poolrooms, and bathrooms with sunken baths—intruding into one chamber where a dishevelled man in pajamas was doing liver exercises on the floor. It was Mr. Klipspringer, the "boarder." I had seen him wandering hungrily about the beach that morning. Finally we came to Gatsby's own apartment, a bedroom and a bath and a Renaissance study, where we sat down and drank a glass of some Chartreuse he took from a cupboard in the wall.

He hadn't once ceased looking at Daisy and I think he revalued everything in his house according to the measure of response it drew from her well-loved eyes. Sometimes, too, he stared around at his possessions in a dazed way as though in her actual and astounding presence none of it was any longer real. Once he nearly toppled down a flight of stairs.

His bedroom was the simplest room of all—except where the dresser was garnished with a toilet set of pure dull gold. Daisy took the brush with delight and smoothed her hair, whereupon Gatsby sat down and shaded his eyes and began to laugh.

"It's the funniest thing," he said hilariously. "I can't—when I try to——"

He had passed visibly through two states and was entering upon a third. After his embarrassment and his unreasoning joy he was consumed with wonder at her presence. He had been full of the idea so long, dreamed it right through to the end, waited with his teeth set, so to speak, at an inconceivable pitch of intensity. Now, in the reaction, he was running down like an overwound clock.

Recovering himself in a minute he opened for us two hulking patent cabinets which held his massed suits and dressing gowns and ties, and his shirts piled like bricks in stacks a dozen high.

"I've got a man in England who buys me clothes. He sends me a bunch of things over at the beginning of each season, spring and fall."

He took out a pile of shirts and began throwing them one by one on the table, shirts of sheer linen and thick silk and fine flannel which lost their folds as they fell and covered the table in many-colored disarray. While we admired he brought more and the soft rich heap mounted higher—shirts with stripes and scrolls and plaids in coral and apple green and lavender and faint orange with monograms of Indian blue. Suddenly with a strained sound Daisy bent her head into the shirts and began to cry stormily.

"They're such beautiful shirts," she sobbed, her voice muffled in the thick folds. "It makes me sad because I've never seen such—such beautiful shirts before."

After the house we were to see the grounds and the swimming pool and the hydroplane and the midsummer flowers—but outside Gatsby's window it began to rain again so we stood in a row looking at the corrugated surface of the Sound.

"If it wasn't for the mist we could see your home across the bay," said Gatsby. "You always have a green light that burns all night at the end of your dock."

Daisy put her arm through his abruptly but he seemed absorbed in what he had just said. Possibly it had occurred to him that the colossal significance of that light had now vanished forever. Compared to the great distance that had separated him from Daisy it had seemed very near to her, almost touching her. It had seemed as close as a star to the moon. Now it was again a green light on a dock. His count of enchanted objects had diminished by one.

I began to walk about the room, examining various indefinite objects in the half darkness. A large photograph of an elderly man in yachting costume attracted me, hung on the wall over his desk.

"Who's this?"

"That? That's Mr. Dan Cody, old sport."

The name sounded faintly familiar.

"He's dead now. He used to be my best friend years ago."

There was a small picture of Gatsby, also in yachting costume, on the bureau—Gatsby with his head thrown back defiantly—taken apparently when he was about eighteen.

"I adore it!" exclaimed Daisy. "The pompadour! You never told me you had a pompadour—or a yacht."

"Look at this," said Gatsby quickly. "Here's a book I kept with clippings—about you."

They stood side by side examining it. I was about to ask to see the rubies when the phone rang and Gatsby took up the receiver.

"I can't talk now. . . . Not today. . . . No, not possibly. . . . All right. Goodbye!"

"Come here *quick!*" cried Daisy at the window.

The rain was still falling, but the darkness had parted in the west, and there was a pink and golden billow of foamy clouds above the sea.

"Look at that," she whispered, and then after a minute: "I'd like just to get one of those clouds and put you in it and push you around."

I tried to go then, but they wouldn't hear of it; perhaps my presence made them feel more satisfactorily alone.

"I know what we'll do," said Gatsby. "We'll have Klipspringer play the piano."

He went out of the room calling "Ewing!" and returned in a few minutes accompanied by an embarrassed, slightly worn young man with shell-rimmed glasses and scanty blond hair. He was decently clothed in a "sport-shirt" open at the neck, sneakers and duck trousers of a nebulous hue.

"Did we interrupt your exercises?" said Daisy politely.

"I was asleep," cried Mr. Klipspringer, in a spasm of embarrassment. "That is, I'd *been* asleep. Then I got up. . . ."

"Klipspringer plays the piano," said Gatsby, cutting him short. "Don't you, Ewing, old sport?"

"I don't play well. I don't—I hardly play at all. I'm all out of prac——"

"We'll go downstairs," interrupted Gatsby. He turned a switch. The grey windows disappeared as the house glowed full of light.

In the music room Gatsby turned on a solitary lamp beside the piano. He lit Daisy's cigarette from a trembling match and sat down with her on a couch far across the room where there was no light save what the gleaming floor bounced in from the hall.

When Klipspringer had played "The Love Nest" he turned around on the bench and searched unhappily for Gatsby in the gloom.

"I'm all out of practice, you see. I told you I couldn't play. I'm all out of prac——"

"Don't talk so much, old sport," commanded Gatsby. "Play!"

> *"In the morning,*
> *In the evening,*
> *Ain't we got fun——"*

Outside the wind was loud and there was a faint flow of thunder along the Sound. All the lights were going on in West Egg now; the electric trains, men-carrying, were plunging home through the rain from New York. It was the hour of a profound human change and excitement was generating on the air.

> *"One thing's sure and nothing's surer*
> *The rich get richer and the poor get—children,*
> *In the meantime,*
> *In between time——"*

As I went over to say goodbye I saw that the expression of bewilderment had come back into Gatsby's face, as though a faint doubt had occurred to him as to the quality of his present happiness. Almost five years! There must have been moments even that afternoon when Daisy tumbled short of his dreams—not through her own fault but because of the colossal vitality of his illusion. It had gone beyond her, beyond everything. He had thrown himself into it with a creative passion, adding to it all the time, decking it out with every bright feather that drifted his way. No amount of fire or freshness could challenge what a man can store up in his ghostly heart.

As I watched him he adjusted himself a little, visibly. His hand took hold of hers and as she said something low in his ear he turned toward her with a rush of emotion. I think that voice held him most with its fluctuating, feverish warmth because it couldn't be over-dreamed—that voice was a deathless song.

They had forgotten me but Daisy glanced up and held out her hand; Gatsby didn't know me now at all. I looked once more at them and they looked back at me, remotely, possessed by intense life. Then I went out of the room and down the marble steps into the rain, leaving them there together.

CHAPTER VI

A few days later somebody brought Tom Buchanan into Gatsby's house for a drink. It seemed strange to me that it hadn't happened before.

It was Sunday afternoon and a party of three on horseback trotted up the drive—Tom and a man named Sloane and a pretty woman in a brown riding habit who had been there before.

"I'm delighted to see you," said Gatsby standing on his porch. "Come right in. I'm delighted that you came."

As though they cared!

"Sit right down. Have a cigarette or a cigar." He walked around the room quickly, ringing bells. "I'll have something to drink for you in just a minute."

He was uneasy because Tom was there. But he would be uneasy anyhow until he had given them something, realizing in a vague way that that was all they came for. Mr. Sloane wanted nothing. A lemonade? No thanks. A little champagne? Nothing at all, thanks. I'm sorry——

"Did you have a nice ride?"

"Very good roads around here."

"I suppose the automobiles——"

"Yeah."

Gatsby turned to Tom who had accepted the introduction as a stranger.

"I believe we've met somewhere before, Mr. Buchanan."

"Oh, yes," said Tom, gruffly polite but obviously not remembering. "So we did. I remember very well."

"About two weeks ago."

"That's right. You were with Nick here."

Gatsby hesitated.

"I know your wife," he said.

"That so?"

Tom turned to me.

"You live near here, Nick?"

"Next door."

"That so?"

Mr. Sloane didn't enter into the conversation but lounged back haughtily in his chair; the woman said nothing either—until unexpectedly, after two highballs, she became cordial.

"We'll all come over to your next party, Mr. Gatsby," she suggested. "What do you say?"

"Certainly. I'd be delighted to have you." He nodded at Tom and at Mr. Sloane.

"Be ver' nice," said Mr. Sloane, without gratitude. "Well—think ought to be starting home."

"Please don't hurry," Gatsby urged them. "Why don't you—why don't you stay for supper? I wouldn't be surprised if some other people dropped in from New York."

"You come to supper with *me*," said the lady enthusiastically. "Both of you."

This included me. Mr. Sloane got to his feet.

"Come along," he said—but to her only.

"I mean it," she insisted. "I'd love to have you. Lots of room."

Gatsby looked at me questioningly. He was eager to go, but Mr. Sloane had evidently determined that he shouldn't.

"I'm afraid I won't be able to," I said.

"Well, you come," she urged, concentrating on Gatsby.

Mr. Sloane murmured something close to her ear.

"We won't be late if we start now," she protested impatiently.

"I haven't got a horse," apologized Gatsby. "I used to ride in the army but I've never bought a horse. I'll have to follow you in my car. Excuse me for just a minute."

The rest of us walked out on the porch where Sloane and the lady began an impassioned conversation aside.

"My God, I believe the man's coming," said Tom. "Doesn't he know she doesn't want him?"

"She says she does."

"She has a big dinner party and he won't know a soul there."

Suddenly Mr. Sloane and the lady walked down the steps and mounted their horses.

"Come on," said Mr. Sloane to Tom, "we're late. We've got to go."

Tom and I shook hands, the rest of us exchanged a cool nod and they trotted quickly down the drive, disappearing under the August foliage just as Gatsby with hat and light overcoat in hand came out of the house.

"They couldn't wait," I told him. "I really don't believe there was room at the table for us. She said she'd call up another time."

"That's funny," he said, with disappointment in his voice. "In fact it seems sort of rude to me."

"It was."

"What's the idea, old sport?"

"They just didn't have room for us, that's all. She was a bit lit and didn't realize it till she got out in the open air."

He sat down, frowning. I think he would have liked to run into Daisy casually as a guest of someone she knew.

"Good looking fellow, isn't he?" he said after a minute.

"Who?"

"Buchanan. Great football player wasn't he?"

"One of the best."

"And a good polo player too?"

"Yes, but they say the ponies he brought east aren't any good, and he's so stubborn he thinks they are."

He was impressed with Tom—that came out in a moment when he spoke of getting a horse.

"I'd like to ride tonight," he said thoughtfully. "I could telephone a barn in New York and have one sent out in a big van."

Whether Tom, seeking new fields of amusement, brought Daisy, or Daisy suggested it to Tom I don't know—they were at Gatsby's house the following Saturday night. The party was a little more elaborate than any of the others; there were two orchestras for example—jazz in the gardens and intermittent "classical stuff" from the veranda above. It was a harvest dance with the immemorial decorations—sheaves of wheat, crossed rakes, and corncobs in geometrical designs—straw knee deep on the floor and a negro dressed as a field hand serving cider, which nobody wanted, at a straw covered bar. The real bar was outside, under a windmill whose blades, studded with colored lights, revolved slowly through the summer air.

Only about a third of the guests were in costume, and this included the orchestra who were dressed as "village constables." As most of the others were village constables also the effect was given that the members of the orchestra got up at intervals and danced with the ladies present—an illusion which added to the pleasant confusion of the scene. For those who came without country costumes straw hats and sunbonnets were provided at the door.

I dislike fancy dress enormously but as the nearest neighbor I cooperated to the extent of a pair of overalls and a grey goatee. The goatee kept getting in my mouth all evening until finally I tore it off ferociously, and much of my chin came with it. I've got a sort of deep dimple in my chin that's always bothered me shaving—it caught in that.

Tom came in a dinner coat, but Daisy, buttoned into a tight Provençal peasant costume, was lovelier than I had ever seen her lovely. Her eyes were bright too and her voice was playing gay murmurous tricks in her throat.

"It's wonderful," she whispered. "These things excite me *so*. If you want to kiss me any time during the evening, Nick, just let me know and I'll be glad to arrange it for you. Just mention my name. Or present a green—or present a green card. I'm giving out green——"

"I thought you'd like it," said Gatsby, his eyes glittering with happiness. "Just look around."

"I know. It's wonderful——"

"I mean the people," he interrupted. "You must see many faces of people you've heard of."

Tom's eyes roved here and there among the guests.

"We don't go round very much," he said. "In fact, I was just thinking that I don't know a soul here."

Gatsby stared at him, first incredulously and then with tolerance.

"I mean their pictures," he explained more formally. "For instance there's——"

In a low voice he began a roster of the more prominent names.

"But it will be a privilege to introduce you," he said. And as we moved off he added, reassuringly: "They're all as natural and unaffected as they can be."

He took us politely from group to group until Tom and Daisy had met everyone of consequence in the garden. Finally we approached the moving picture celebrity whom I had seen there before. She was surrounded by at least a dozen men who from a distance seemed to be making violent love to her. Coming closer, however, we discovered that the men were some less important members of the moving picture profession, and that their attitude was one of marked respect. They swayed toward her, not with passion, but lest they miss one of the jokes to which she was addicted, and which they applauded with hilarious laughter. Through this reverent entourage Gatsby made way.

"Mrs. Buchanan—" he introduced her, "and Mr. Buchanan—" after an instant's hesitation he added, "the polo player."

"Oh, no," said Tom quickly. "Not me."

However the sound of it evidently pleased Gatsby, and Tom remained "the polo player" throughout the rest of the tour.

"I've never met so many grand celebrities before," said Daisy. "I like that man, what was his name, with the sort of blue nose——"

"Augustus Waize," said Gatsby. "Oh, he's just a small producer. He only does one play a year."

"I liked him anyhow. And it must be fascinating to know them all."

"They like to come here," he admitted, "and I enjoy having them."

"I'd a little rather not be the polo player," said Tom pleasantly. "I'd rather look at all these famous people in—in oblivion."

He meant incognito but in any case Gatsby was surprised. He felt that in placing Tom, in attesting him as a spectacular figure among these other spectacular figures, he had done him a service.

Daisy and Gatsby danced; it was the first time I had ever seen him dance. Formally, with neither awkwardness nor grace, he moved at a conservative foxtrot around the platform. They were both very solemn about it, as if it were a sort of rite—perhaps they were thinking of some other summer night when they had danced together back in the old, sad, poignant days of the war. Once she looked up at him in such a way that I glanced sharply around to see if Tom were watching. But he'd found amusement elsewhere— he was bringing some girl a cocktail from the bar.

When the music stopped Daisy and Gatsby strolled over to me.

"Where's Tom?" she inquired. Then she saw: "Oh—well, don't let's disturb him. She's pretty, isn't she. Common but——"

She stopped herself suddenly but Gatsby was occupied in looking around the garden.

"There's several other people I want you to meet," he said, "but one of them hasn't arrived yet."

"We'll wait till they all get here," she suggested. "We'll leave Nick here in case there's a fire or a flood or anything and wander around. You'll tell us, Nick, in case there's a fire or a flood—or any act of God? We insured the house last week and I remember——"

The tumultuous clamor, like a prolongation of the nervous sounds of New York, soothed me, and I felt at home. But I tried to imagine how the party would appear to Daisy, how it had appeared to me on that June night two months before. It seemed less bizarre now—it seemed a world complete in itself, with its own standards and its own great figures, bounded, to its own satisfaction, by its own wall. It was second to nothing because it had no consciousness of being so. But Daisy might well regard it as the preposterous and rather sinister fringe of the universe.

"Listen, Nick——" She was back beside me. "Would you mind if we went over and sat on the steps of your bungalow or whatever it is?"

"You and Tom?"

"No, Jay and me."

She never saw any humor except her own—not always that.

"It's so noisy here," she explained, "and I have this ear drum, you see. I thought if we sat on your steps I'd get all—— What's that girl yelling about?"

"She's tight and she has hysterics."

"Oh! . . . Well, we want to sit on your steps." She hesitated. "If Tom starts paging me around the garden you'll come and tell us won't you. I wouldn't want him to think I was bad."

She winked solemnly and I began to laugh as she went back toward the house.

An hour later Tom asked me casually if I'd seen Daisy; I sent him inside. Crossing the two lawns I found them sitting on the steps in the bright moonlight.

"Nick," she called.

"Yes."

"We're having a row."

"What about?"

"Oh, about things," she replied vaguely. "About the future—the future of the black race. My theory is we've got to beat them down."

"You don't know what you want," said Gatsby suddenly.

She didn't answer. Without haste we strolled back over the dark lawn to the area of hilarity, and Daisy and I danced. Gatsby made a complete circuit of the garden, speaking to people here and there, and then stood alone for a while in his habitual place on the steps.

"Do you think I'm making a mistake?" asked Daisy, leaning back and looking up into my face.

"I don't understand."

"Well, I'm going to leave Tom."

I was illogically startled.

"Do you mean immediately?"

"No. When I'm ready. When it can be arranged." Her eyes were sincere, her voice was full and sad.

"Have you told Tom?"

"No, not yet. I'm not going to do anything for a month or two. Then I'll decide."

"I thought you'd decided."

"Yes, but—then I'll decide the details and all that." She laughed. "You know if you've never gone through a thing like this it's not so easy. In fact—I want to just go, and not tell Tom anything.

"Do you think I'm making a mistake?"

"I don't know Gatsby well," I said cautiously. "I like him, but I'm not competent to give advice."

"He's wonderful," she said confidently.

As we sat down at a table I found that I was illogically depressed at what she had told me. These break-ups, however justified, however wise, always have a tragic irony of their own.

Supper was being served. Gatsby joined us at the table and, discovering us, Tom came across the garden.

"Mind if I sit with some people over here?" he inquired. "It's that man with the blue nose. He's been getting off some funny stuff."

"Go right ahead," said Daisy genially. "If you want to take down any more addresses here's my gold pencil."

Tom laughed and hurried away.

Gatsby, who had been talking to the moving picture celebrity, remarked suddenly that she had been very complimentary about Daisy. His voice was proud and pleased.

"And, here's a chance to become famous—she wants to know where you got your hair cut."

"You tell her I think she's lovely too," said Daisy pleasantly.

Gatsby took out a pencil and a notebook.

"Where do you get your hair cut? I promised her I'd ask you."

"It's a secret," whispered Daisy. "It's a man I discovered myself and I wouldn't tell anybody for the world."

"You don't understand," he said impressively. "She'll probably have hers done the same way and you'll be the originator of a new vogue all over the country."

"No thanks," said Daisy lightly. The disappointment in his face bothered her, and she added: "Do you think I want that person to go around with her hair cut exactly like mine? It'd spoil it for me."

Without a word Gatsby replaced the notebook in his pocket.

"We're together here in your garden, Jay—your beautiful garden," broke out Daisy suddenly. "It doesn't seem possible, does it? I can't believe it's possible. Will you have somebody look up in the encyclopedia and see if it's really true. Look it up under G."

For a moment I thought this was casual chatter—then I realized that she was trying to drown out from us, from herself, a particularly obscene conversation that four women were carrying on at a table just behind.

"I thought if we ever met it'd be when we were old—and decrepit——" She broke off and glanced around in a frightened way. "What is it?" she whispered. "Why is that woman acting like that? Is she drunk?"

"I think you're probably nervous," said Gatsby. "She's just having a good time." He hesitated. "I don't know what's the matter tonight; very few people seem to be enjoying themselves."

Her wandering eyes caught his and perceived his disappointment.

"Why, they are, Jay," she cried quickly. "Everybody's having a wonderful time. Have I said something that you—here——!"

With her little gold pencil she wrote an address on the tablecloth. "There's where I get my hair cut. Is that what she wanted to know?"

But there was no such intimacy between them as would allow them to criticize each other's friends. Gatsby took out his pencil and slowly obliterated her markings with his own.

At one o'clock we sat on the moonlit front steps waiting for Gatsby to come and say goodbye.

"Who is our host anyhow?" inquired Tom. "Some big bootlegger?"

"Be quiet!" Daisy warned him sharply. "You have no reason for talking like that."

"Well—" Tom yawned placidly, "he certainly went into the highways and byways to get this crowd together."

"At least they accomplish something. They're more interesting than—the people we see."

"You didn't look so interested."

"Well, I was," she asserted stoutly. "I was having a marvellous time."

Tom laughed scoffingly.

"Did you see Daisy's face when that girl wanted her to put her to bed?"

Daisy began to sing in a low voice, resolutely disregarding him; then, frowning, she broke off and made a sudden attempt to separate Gatsby from his party.

"Lots of people come who haven't been invited," she said. "He told me so himself. That girl who was so—so funny hadn't been invited. They simply force their way in and he's too kind to object." She hesitated. "Of course he's much nicer than the people he entertains."

"He's just like them," said Tom.

"Be quiet!"

Gatsby was coming down the steps. With exaggerated enthusiasm Daisy thanked him for their good time.

"I suppose it'll last quite late," she said.

"Oh, yes. Some time longer."

She got into the limousine.

"Good night——" Her lips formed the word "dear," her fingers just brushed the back of his hand. Tom, his eyes closed sleepily, was already leaning back in a corner of the car.

"Good night," repeated Daisy. Her glance left Gatsby and sought the lighted top of the steps where a contralto song was drifting out the open door. After all in the very casualness of Gatsby's party there were romantic possibilities totally absent from her world. What was it up there in the song that seemed to be calling him back inside? What would happen now in the dim, incalculable hours? Perhaps some unbelievable guest would arrive—a person infinitely rare and to be marvelled at, who would never be seen anywhere again . . . or perhaps some authentically radiant young girl who with one fresh glance at Gatsby, one moment of magical encounter, would blot out those five years of unwavering devotion.

As the car moved off a flush of apprehension made her stretch out her hand, trying to touch his once more.

CHAPTER VII

It was about this time that an ambitious young reporter from New York arrived at Gatsby's door one morning and asked him if he had anything to say.

"Anything to say about what?" inquired Gatsby politely.

"Why—any statement to give out."

It transpired after a confused five minutes that the man had heard Gatsby's name around his office in a connection which he either wouldn't reveal or didn't fully understand. It was his day off and with laudable initiative he had hurried out "to see."

It was an accident, and yet the reporter's instinct was right. Gatsby's notoriety, spread about by the hundreds who had accepted his hospitality and thus become authorities on his past, had increased all summer until he fell just short of being news. Contemporary legends such as the "underground pipe-line to Canada" attached themselves to him, and there was one persistent story that he didn't live in a house at all but in a boat that looked like a house and was moved secretly up and down the Long Island shore. It was when curiosity was at the highest about him that his lights failed to go on one Saturday night—and as obscurely as it had begun his career as Trimalchio suddenly ended.

For several weeks I hadn't seen him and I perceived gradually that the automobiles that turned expectantly into his drive stayed only a minute and then drove rather sulkily away. Wondering if he were ill I went over to find out—an unfamiliar butler with a villainous face squinted at me suspiciously from the open door.

"Is Mr. Gatsby ill?"

"Nope," he answered, adding "sir" in a dilatory, grudging way.

"I hadn't seen him and I was rather worried. Tell him Mr. Carraway came over from next door."

"Who?" he demanded rudely.

"Carraway."

"Carraway. All right, I'll tell him."

Abruptly he slammed the door.

It was my Finn who informed me that Gatsby had dismissed every servant in his house a week ago and replaced them with half a dozen others who never went into the village and who never exchanged a word with the tradesmen except to order supplies over the telephone. The grocery boy reported that the kitchen looked like a pigsty and the general opinion in the village was that the new people weren't servants at all.

After that I watched for Gatsby, and found him several evenings later, coming across my own lawn. He had lost a little of his tan and his eyes were bright and tired. We sat down on a bench in the yard.

"Going away?" I asked.

"No, old sport. Why?"

"I hear you fired all your servants."

He hesitated.

"Daisy comes over sometimes in the afternoon. And I wanted some people who wouldn't gossip—until we decide what we're going to do. These two towns are pretty close together."

"Where'd you find these?" I inquired, determined to show no curiosity about Daisy.

"They're some people Wolfshiem wanted to do something for," he said vaguely. "They're all brothers and sisters—they used to run a small hotel. What's the difference, so long as they can cook and make beds?"

This was a new note from Gatsby, whose household had been exemplary in its own extravagant way.

"You're depressed," I remarked.

"I'm very sad, old sport." He hesitated. "Daisy wants us to run off together. She came over this afternoon with a suitcase all packed and ready in the car." Gatsby shook his head wearily. "I tried to explain to her that we couldn't do that, and I only made her cry."

"In other words you've got her—and now you don't want her."

"Of course I want her," he exclaimed in horror. "Why—Daisy's all I've got left from a world so wonderful that to think of it makes me sick all over." He looked around him in wild regret. "But we mustn't just run away like we might have done five years ago," he said after a pause. "That won't do at all."

He seemed to feel that Daisy should make some sort of atonement that would give her love the value that it had before. Anyone might have come along in a few years and taken her away from Tom—he wanted this to have an element of fate about it, of inevitability—the resumption of an interrupted dance. And first Daisy must purify herself by a renunciation of the years between.

"But how can she do that?" I asked, puzzled.

"She can go to her husband and tell him that she never loved him. She can set that much right. Then we can go back to Louisville and be married in her house and start life over."

He jumped up and began walking back and forth frantically, as if the past that he wanted to repeat were lurking here under the very shadow of his house, just out of reach of his hand. His impassioned sentimentality possessed him so thoroughly that he seemed to be in some fantastic communication with space and time—and they must have given him his answer then and there in the moonlight, for he sat down suddenly and put his face in his hands and began to sob.

"I beg your pardon, old sport," he said chokingly, "but it's all so sad because I can't make her understand."

I began patting him idiotically on the back, and presently he sat back and began to stare at his house.

"She even wants to leave that," he said bitterly. "I've gotten these things for her, and now she wants to run away."

"Take what you can get, Gatsby," I urged him. "Daisy's a person—she's not just a figure in your dream. And she probably doesn't feel that she owes you anything at all."

"She does, though. Why—I'm only thirty-two. I might be a great man if I could forget that once I lost Daisy. But my career has got to be like this——" He drew a slanting line from the lawn to the stars. "It's got to keep going up. I used to think wonderful things were going to happen to me, before I met her. And I knew it was a great mistake for a man like me to fall in love—and then one night I let myself go, and it was too late——"

They had been walking together down the street one autumn night five years ago when the leaves were falling, and they came to a place where there were no trees and the sidewalk was white with moonlight. They stopped here and turned toward each other. Now it was a cool night with that mysterious excitement in it which comes at the two changes of the year. The quiet lights in the houses were humming out in the darkness and there was a sort of stir and bustle among the stars. Out of the corner of his eye Gatsby saw that the blocks of the sidewalk really formed a ladder and mounted to a secret place above the trees—he could climb to it, if he climbed alone, and once there he could suck on the pap of life, gulp down the incomparable milk of wonder.

His heart beat faster and faster as Daisy's white face came up to his own. He knew that when he kissed this girl, and forever wed his unutterable visions to her perishable breath, his mind would never romp again like the mind of God. So he waited, listening for a moment longer to the tuning-fork that had been struck upon a star. Then he kissed her. At his lips' touch she blossomed for him like a flower and the incarnation was complete.

Through all he said, even through his appalling sentimentality, I was reminded of something—an elusive rhythm, a fragment of lost words that I had heard somewhere a long time ago. For a moment a phrase tried to take shape in my mouth and my lips parted like a dumb man's, as though there was more struggling upon them than a wisp of startled air. But they made no sound and what I had almost remembered was incommunicable forever.

The thirtieth of August was a half holiday and I had promised Tom Buchanan to have lunch with them at East Egg. Daisy had invited "that man Gatsby" and Tom didn't know how they could go through with it unless I'd come over too.

It was a broiling day, almost the last, certainly the hottest of the summer. As the train emerged from the tunnel into sunlight the hot whistles of the National Biscuit Company broke the simmering hush of noon. The straw seats of the car hovered on the edge of combustion; the woman next to me perspired delicately for awhile into her white shirtwaist and then, as her newspaper dampened under her fingers, lapsed despairingly into deep heat with a desolate cry, her pocket-book slapping to the floor.

"Oh, *my!*" she gasped.

I picked it up with a weary bend and handed it back to her. I held it at arm's length and by the extreme tip of the corners to indicate that I had no designs upon it—but everyone nearby, including the woman, suspected me just the same.

"Hot!" said the conductor to familiar faces. "Some weather! . . . Hot! . . . Hot! . . . Hot! . . . Is it hot enough for you? Is it hot? Is it . . . ?"

My commutation ticket came back to me with a dark stain from his hand. That anyone should care in this heat whose flushed lips he kissed, whose head made damp the pajama pocket over his heart!

. . . Through the hall of the Buchanans' house blew a faint wind, carrying the sound of the telephone bell out to Gatsby and me as we waited at the door.

"The master's body!" roared the butler into the mouthpiece. "I'm sorry madame but we can't furnish it—it's far too hot to touch this noon!"

What he really said was "Yes . . . . Yes . . . . I'll see."

Then he set down the receiver and came toward us, glistening slightly, to take our stiff straw hats.

"Madame expects you in the salon!" he cried, needlessly indicating the door. In this heat every extra gesture was an affront to the common store of life.

The room, shadowed well with awnings, was dark and cool. Daisy and Jordan lay upon an enormous couch, like silver idols, weighing down their own white dresses against the singing breeze of the fans.

"We can't move," they said together.

Jordan's fingers, powdered white over their tan, lay for a moment in mine.

"And Mr. Thomas Buchanan, the athlete?" I inquired.

Simultaneously I heard his voice, gruff, muffled, husky, at the hall telephone.

Gatsby stood in the center of the crimson carpet and gazed

around with fascinated eyes. Daisy watched him and laughed her sweet exciting laugh; a tiny gust of powder rose from her bosom into the air.

"The rumor is," whispered Jordan, "that that's Tom's girl on the telephone."

We were silent. The voice in the hall rose high with annoyance. "Very well then, I won't sell you the car at all. . . . I'm under no obligations to you at all. . . . And as far as your bothering me about it at lunch time I won't stand that at all!"

"Holding down the receiver," said Daisy cynically.

"No, he's not," I assured her. "It's a verbatim deal. I happen to know about it."

Tom flung open the door, blocked out its space for a moment with his thick body, and hurried into the room.

"Mr. Gatsby!" He put out his broad, flat hand. "I'm glad to see you, sir. . . . Nick. . . . "

"Make us a cold drink," cried Daisy.

As he left the room she got up and went over to Gatsby, and pulled his face down kissing him on the mouth.

"I love you," she murmured proudly.

"You forget that there's a lady present," said Jordan.

Daisy looked around doubtfully.

"You kiss Nick too."

"What a low, vulgar girl!"

"I don't care!" cried Daisy and began to clog on the brick fireplace. Then she remembered the heat and sat down guiltily on the couch just as a freshly laundered nurse leading a little girl came into the room.

"Bles-sed prec-ious," she crooned, holding out her arms. "Come to your own mother that loves you."

The child, relinquished by the nurse, rushed across the room and rooted shyly into her mother's dress.

"The bles-sed prec-ious! Did mother get powder on your old yellowy hair? Stand up now, and say How-de-do."

Gatsby and I in turn leaned down and took the small reluctant hand. Afterward he kept looking at the child with a sort of surprise. I don't think he had really ever believed in its existence before.

"I got dressed before luncheon," said the child, turning eagerly to Daisy.

"That's because your mother wanted to show you off." Her face bent into the single wrinkle of the small white neck. "You dream, you. You absolute little dream."

"Yes," admitted the child calmly. "Aunt Jordan's got on a white dress too."

"How do you like mother's friends?" Daisy turned her around so that she faced Gatsby. "Do you think they're pretty?"

"Where's Daddy?"

"She doesn't look like her father," explained Daisy. "She looks like me. She's got my hair and shape of the face. I'm glad of that."

Tom came back into the room preceded by four gin rickeys that clicked full of ice.

"What did you say?" he demanded. "That Pammy doesn't look like me?"

"Well, she doesn't. She looks just like me."

"I know. But you say it as if she'd escaped some curse. What's the idea?"

Daisy sat back upon the couch. The nurse took a step forward and held out her hand.

"Come Pammy."

"Goodbye, sweetheart!"

With a reluctant backward glance the well-disciplined child held to her nurse's hand and was pulled out the door.

Gatsby took up his drink.

"They certainly look cool," he said with visible tension.

We drank in long greedy swallows.

"I read somewhere that the sun's getting hotter every year," said Tom genially. "It seems that pretty soon the earth's going to fall into the sun—or wait a minute—it's just the opposite—the sun's getting colder every year.

"Come outside," he suggested to Gatsby. "I'd like you to have a look at the place."

I went with them out to the veranda. On the green Sound, stagnant in the heat, one small sail crawled slowly toward the fresher sea. Gatsby's eyes followed it momentarily; he raised his hand and pointed across the bay.

"I'm right across from you."

"So you are."

Our eyes lifted over the rosebeds and the hot lawn and the weedy refuse of the dog days along shore. Slowly the white wings of the boat moved against the blue cool limit of the sky. Ahead lay the scalloped ocean and the abounding blessed isles.

"There's sport for you," said Tom, nodding. "I'd like to be out there with him for about an hour."

We had luncheon in the dining room, darkened, too, against the heat, and drank down nervous gayety with the cold ale.

"What'll we do with ourselves this afternoon?" cried Daisy, "and the day after that, and the next thirty years?"

"Don't be morbid," Jordan said. "Life starts all over again when it gets crisp in the fall."

"But it's so hot," insisted Daisy, on the verge of tears, "and everything's so confused. Let's all go to town!"

Her voice struggled on through the heat, beating against it, moulding its senselessness into forms.

"I've heard of making a garage out of a stable," Tom was saying to Gatsby, "but I'm the first man who ever made a stable out of a garage."

"Who wants to go to town?" demanded Daisy insistently. Gatsby's eyes floated toward her. "Ah," she cried, "you look so cool."

Their eyes met, and they stared together at each other, alone in space. With an effort she glanced down at the table.

"You always look so cool," she repeated.

She had told him that she loved him, and Tom Buchanan saw. He was astounded. His mouth opened a little and he looked at her and then at Gatsby and then back at Daisy as if he had just recognized her as someone he knew a long time ago.

"You look like the advertisement of the man," she went on innocently. "You know the advertisement of the man——"

"All right," broke in Tom quickly, "I'm perfectly willing to go to town. Come on—we're all going to town."

He got up, his eyes still flashing between Gatsby and his wife. No one moved.

"Come on!" His temper cracked a little. "What's the matter anyhow? If we're going to town let's start."

His hand, trembling with his effort at self control, bore to his lips the last of his glass of ale. Daisy's voice got us to our feet and out onto the blazing gravel drive.

"Are we just going to *go?*" she objected. "Like this? Aren't we going to let anyone smoke a cigarette first?"

"Everybody smoked all through lunch," said Tom truculently.

"Oh, let's have fun," she begged him. "It's too hot to fuss."

Tom didn't answer. She decided suddenly that it was best to go.

"Come on, Jordan."

They went upstairs to get ready while we three men stood there shuffling the hot pebbles with our feet. A silver curve of the moon hovered already in the western sky.

"Have you got your stables here?" asked Gatsby.

"About a quarter of a mile down the road."

"Oh."

A pause.

"I don't see the idea of going to town," broke out Tom savagely. "Women get these ideas in their heads——"

"Shall we take anything to drink?" called Daisy from an upper window.

"I'll get some whiskey," answered Tom. He went inside.

Gatsby turned to me, his voice trembling.

"I can't stand this," he said, "it's agony. I wanted to put my arms around her at luncheon when he began that talk. She's got to tell him the truth."

"She loves you. Her voice is full of it."

"Her voice is full of money," he said suddenly.

That was it. I had never understood before. It was full of money—that was the inexhaustible charm that rose and fell in it, the jingle of it, the cymbals' song of it. . . . High in a white palace the king's daughter, the golden girl. . . .

Tom came out of the house wrapping a quart bottle in a towel, followed by Daisy and Jordan wearing small tight hats of metallic cloth and carrying light capes over their arms.

"Shall we all go in my car?" suggested Gatsby. He felt the hot green leather of the seat. "I should have left it in the shade."

"Standard shift?" asked Tom, looking at him quickly.

"Yes."

"Well, you take my coupé and let me drive your car to town."

"Of course, if you like to," said Gatsby stiffly. "I don't know how much gas there is——"

"Come on, Daisy!" Tom slipped his hand around her waist. "I'll take you in this circus wagon."

He opened the door for her but she moved out from the circle of his arm.

"Nick and Jordan'll go with you," she said lightly. "I'll take Gatsby for a thriller in the coupé."

She stood close to Gatsby, touching his coat with her hand. Unwillingly Tom got into the yellow car, making room for Jordan and me in the front seat. He pushed the unfamiliar gears tentatively, and we moved off toward the city through the oppressive afternoon while they followed far out of sight behind.

"I wonder where that man Gatsby learned his manners," broke out Tom suddenly.

"He went to Oxford," said Jordan maliciously. "Ever hear of it?"

"He did!" Tom was incredulous. "Like hell he did! He wears a pink suit."

"Nevertheless he's an Oxford man."

"Oxford, South Dakota," snorted Tom contemptuously, "Oxford, New Mexico, or something like that."

"Listen, Tom, if you're such a snob why did you invite him to lunch?" demanded Jordan crossly.

"Daisy invited him. She knew him before we were married— God knows where!"

We were all irritable now with the fading ale and, aware of it, we drove for awhile in silence. Then as Dr. T. J. Eckleburg's faded eyes came into sight down the road I remembered Gatsby's caution about gasoline.

"We've got half a gallon," said Tom carelessly, glancing at the gauge. "That'll probably get us to town."

"But there's a garage right here," objected Jordan. "I don't want to get stalled in this baking heat."

Tom threw on both brakes angrily and we slid to an abrupt dusty stop under Wilson's sign. After a moment the proprietor emerged from the interior of his establishment and gazed hollow-eyed at the car.

"Let's have some gas!" cried Tom boisterously. "What do you think we stopped for—to admire the view?"

"I'm sick," said Wilson without moving. "I've been sick all day."

"What's the matter?"

"I'm all run down."

"Well, shall I help myself?" demanded Tom impatiently. "You sounded well enough on the phone."

With an effort Wilson left the shade and support of the doorway and, breathing hard, unscrewed the cap of the tank. In the sunlight his face was green.

"I didn't mean to interrupt your lunch," he said. "But I need money pretty bad and I was wondering what you were going to do with your old car."

"How do you like this one?" inquired Tom. "I bought it last week."

"It's a nice yellow one," answered Wilson, straining at the handle.

"Like to buy it?"

"Big chance," Wilson smiled faintly. "No, but I could make some money on the other."

"What do you want money for all of a sudden?"

"I've been here too long. I want to get away. My wife and I want to go west."

"Your wife does!" exclaimed Tom, startled.

"She's been talking about it for ten years." He rested for a moment against the pump, shading his eyes. "And now she's going whether she wants to or not. I'm going to get her away."

The coupé flashed by us with a flurry of dust and the flash of a waving hand.

"What do I owe you?" demanded Tom harshly.

"I just got wised up to something funny the last two days," remarked Wilson. "That's why I want to get away. That's why I've been bothering you about the car."

"What do I owe you?"

"Dollar twenty."

It was evident that so far Wilson's suspicions hadn't alighted on Tom. He had discovered that Myrtle had some sort of life apart from him in another world and the shock had made him physically sick. I looked at him and then at Tom, who had made a parallel discovery less than an hour before—and it occurred to me that there was no difference between men, in intelligence or race, so profound as the difference between the sick and the well. Wilson was so sick that he looked guilty, unforgivably guilty—as if he had just got some poor girl with child.

"I'll let you have that car," said Tom. "I'll send it over tomorrow afternoon."

That locality always filled me with vague disquiet even in the broad glare of afternoon and now I turned my head as though I had been warned of something behind. Over the ashheaps the giant eyes of Dr. T. J. Eckleburg kept their vigil but I perceived, after a moment, that other eyes were regarding us with peculiar intensity from less than twenty feet away.

In one of the windows over the garage the curtains had been moved aside a little and Myrtle Wilson was peering down at the car. So engrossed was she that she had no consciousness of being observed and one emotion after another crept into her face like objects into a slowly developing picture. Her expression was curiously familiar—it was an expression I had often seen on women's faces, but on Myrtle Wilson's face it seemed purposeless and inexplicable until I realized that her eyes, wide with jealous terror, were fixed not on Tom but on Jordan Baker, whom she took to be his wife.

There is no confusion like the confusion of a simple mind and as we drove away Tom was feeling the hot whips of panic. His wife and his mistress, until an hour ago secure and inviolate, were slipping precipitately from his control. Instinct made him step on the accelerator with the double purpose of overtaking Daisy and leaving Wilson behind, and we sped along toward Astoria at fifty miles an hour until, among the iron girders of the elevated, we came in sight of the easygoing blue coupé.

"Those big movies around Fiftieth Street are cool," suggested Jordan. "Anyhow, I love New York on hot summer afternoons when everyone's away. There's something very sensuous about it— overripe, as if all sorts of funny fruits were going to fall into your hands."

This had the effect of further disquieting Tom but before he could invent a protest the coupé came to a stop and Daisy's hand signalled us to draw up alongside.

"Where are we going?" Daisy cried.

"The movies I suppose."

"It's so hot," she complained. "You go. We'll ride around and meet you after."

"We can't argue about it here," said Tom impatiently, as a truck gave out a cursing whistle behind us. "You follow me to the south side of Central Park, in front of the Plaza."

Several times he turned his head and looked back for their car, and if the traffic delayed them he slowed up until they came into sight. I think he was afraid they would dart down a side street and out of his life forever.

"Women are funny people," he exclaimed, as we reached the Plaza. "By God, they'll do anything for a little excitement."

After a moment the coupé rolled by us with insolent leisure and parked ahead. Daisy and Gatsby showed no tendency to move so we got out and went up to them, and immediately the Buchanans were engaged in a restrained discussion as to who had suggested the trip to New York. Jordan and I bought popcorn at the park gate and sat munching it on the low wall.

"It was a mistake to come," she remarked. "It looks like a row to me."

We waited. It was so hot that truck-horses left deep hoof-prints in the pavement, so hot that my underwear kept climbing like a damp snake around my legs and intermittent beads of sweat raced cool across my back. There was something special about the day that I kept trying to remember, some anniversary or an important thing that I should do. But it hid itself persistently in the overpowering heat.

"Come on over!" called Daisy. "Everybody's got to help decide. Tom says I haven't any common sense."

We went over to the car.

"The nearest place is the Plaza," she continued facetiously. "We can take a room there and go to sleep. Or else we could engage five tiled bathrooms and take cold baths."

Tom was thoughtful for a moment.

"I'll tell you," he said. "We'll get a room there and have a mint julep and talk it over."

"Talk what over?" asked Daisy uneasily.

"What we're going to do." And he added casually, "Or whatever's on your mind."

"But I don't want to take a room. I think it's the silliest thing I ever——"

"Whether you want to or not, that's what we're going to do," he interrupted grimly.

Gatsby looked questioningly at Daisy.

"If you don't want to——"

"She wants to," said Tom. "And I'm quite able to talk to her myself."

Daisy glanced quickly from one to the other, perceiving to her dismay that things had slipped a little. To avoid an immediate scene she must enclose herself and Gatsby into the same room with Tom for the afternoon.

"You come too," she appealed to Jordan.

"It's an insane idea," I said, but this came too late. I had only to look at Tom and Gatsby to see that it was too late. We took a sitting room on the tenth floor of the Plaza Hotel.

The room was large and stifling, and opening the windows admitted only a gust of hot shrubbery from the Park. Daisy went to the mirror and stood with her back to us fixing her hair.

"It's a swell suite," whispered Jordan respectfully, and everyone laughed. Our secondary preoccupation was with the conviction that this was all very funny.

"Open another window," commanded Daisy, without turning around.

"There aren't any more."

"Well, we'd better put one in. We'd better telephone for an axe——"

Tom unrolled the bottle of whiskey from the concealing towel and set it on the table, and simultaneously the portentous melody of Mendelssohn's "Wedding March" began to float up to the window. There was a wedding in the ballroom below. We listened and presently the music faded to low chords as the ceremony began.

"Do you recognize it Daisy?" Tom inquired. "On the day they played it for us I didn't suspect that you were so devoid of common sense."

"Why not let her alone?" said Gatsby, not unpleasantly. "It was you who insisted we come to town."

There was a moment's silence. The telephone book slipped from its nail and splashed to the floor, whereupon Jordan whispered "Excuse me," and we all laughed again.

"I'll pick it up," I offered.

"I've got it." Gatsby examined the parted string, muttered "Hum!" in an interested way and tossed it on a chair.

"Mr. Gatsby," said Tom. "Sometime I'd like to have a few words with you alone."

"Just as you say, old sport."

Tom laughed without smiling.

"That's a great expression of yours, isn't it?"

"What is?"

"All this 'old sport' business. Where'd you pick that up?"

"Now see here, Tom," said Daisy, turning around from the mirror. "If you're going to be rude and unpleasant I'm not going to stay here a minute, do you understand? I'm going to walk right out of here and go to—and go to a movie. You call up and order some ice and things for your mint julep. That's what we came here for."

As Tom picked up the phone a long cheer drifted in from the

ballroom followed by intermittent cries of "Yea-ea-ea!" and finally by a burst of jazz as the dancing began. Hilariously we danced, Daisy and I, Gatsby and Jordan, while Tom at the telephone watched us with unrestful eyes.

"I want to get out," whispered Daisy. "Can't you fix it? If Tom has much to drink I don't know what he'll do."

I tried and so did Jordan. We tried intermittently for an hour, and perhaps we might have succeeded had not Gatsby inopportunely decided to try himself. He pointedly disregarded Tom and turned to me.

"Let's go, old sport. There's no reason why we should swelter up in this room."

We all got up except Tom.

"Wait a minute," Tom said quietly. "Before we go I want to ask Mr. Gatsby one question."

"Well?"

"What kind of a row are you trying to cause in my house anyhow?"

We all stood there perfectly still. Gatsby was a little pale but there was a joyous exaltation in his eyes as though he were glad it was to happen at last.

"He isn't causing a row," said Daisy. "You're causing a row. Please have a little self control."

"Self control!" repeated Tom incredulously. "I suppose the latest thing is to sit back and let Mr. Nobody from Nowhere make love to your wife. Well, if that's the idea you can count me out. . . . Nowadays people begin by sneering at family life and family institutions and next they'll throw everything overboard and have intermarriage between black and white."

Flushed with his impassioned gibberish he forgot Daisy for a moment and saw himself standing alone on the last barrier of civilization.

"We're all white here," murmured Jordan. "Except possibly Tom."

"Oh, I know I'm not very popular. I don't give big parties. I suppose you've got to make your house into a pigsty in order to have any friends—in the modern world."

Angry as I was, as we all were, I was tempted to laugh whenever he opened his mouth. The transition from libertine to prig was so complete.

"We can talk about my house later," said Gatsby steadily, "when there are no ladies present. What I want to——"

"Who are you anyhow?" broke out Tom. "You're one of that bunch that hang around with Meyer Wolfshiem—that much I happen to know."

"I won't stand this," cried Daisy. "Oh, please let's go out. I want to go home."

"All right," Tom agreed, and for a moment I thought she was going to get him away. "Just as soon as he realizes that his presumptuous little flirtation is over."

Averting her eyes from both of them Daisy moved toward the door and Jordan and I followed.

"Wait a minute, Daisy," Gatsby said. "He calls it a presumptuous little flirtation. . . . Is it?"

She looked around helplessly.

"Is it?" he repeated.

She wanted to evade the question but even for that it was too late.

"No," she admitted in a low voice.

At this point Jordan and I tried to go. Human sympathy has its curious limits and we were repelled by their self absorption, appalled by their conflicting desires. But we were called back by a look in Daisy's eyes which seemed to say: "You have a certain responsibility for all this too." Tom and Gatsby considered that we were leaving out of delicacy. They both insisted with competitive eagerness that we remain, as though neither of them had anything to conceal and it would be a privilege to partake vicariously of their emotions.

Tom made a small O with his mouth and leaned back in his chair, tapping his thick fingers together like a clergyman while his shining arrogant eyes darted at each of us in turn.

"Sit down, Daisy," he said with an unsuccessful attempt at the paternal note. "What's been going on? I want to know."

We all sat down again.

"I'll tell you," Gatsby's eyes met Tom's. "Your wife doesn't love you. Do you Daisy?"

"No." Her answer was almost inaudible.

"Why of course she does!" exclaimed Tom.

Even Gatsby wasn't satisfied with her answer.

"Please say right out whether you love him or not."

"I don't love him."

But her reluctance was so perceptible that Gatsby stood up as if he had been betrayed.

"I don't understand you," he said with less confidence. "I didn't know there was any doubt about it." No one spoke. "If there is, of course—I'll go away."

That there should be the faintest reluctance in Daisy's admission had so startled him that he took a step toward the door.

"Oh, don't go!" she cried in distress. "I love you too."

He turned slowly around, his face wrinkling up, his eyes opening and closing rapidly.

"You love me *too*," he repeated.

"I didn't mean that."

The assertion was too shocking, too incredible for him to grasp—it slipped away from him as he clutched with relief at its retraction.

"Of course Daisy loves me," said Tom with gruff assurance. "The trouble is she doesn't know it. Sometimes she gets foolish ideas in her head, that's all." He nodded sagely. "And I love Daisy too. Once in awhile I go off on a spree and make a fool of myself but I always come back and in my heart I love her all the time."

"You're revolting," said Daisy. Her voice fell an octave lower and filled the room with thrilling scorn.

But now that Tom knew that this was no obscure blow at him from a revengeful heaven, but only a comprehensible phenomenon of desire his confidence reasserted itself.

"You came near making a serious mistake, Daisy. It's a good thing I found out in time."

"Why should you care?" she demanded.

"Of course I care. And I'm going to take better care of you from now on."

"You don't understand," Gatsby said excitedly. "You're not going to take care of her any more."

"Really?" Tom opened his eyes wide and laughed. He could afford to control himself now. "Why not?"

"Because she's leaving you."

"Nonsense."

"I am, though," said Daisy with a visible effort.

Tom considered, looking from one to the other and finding the idea incredible.

"Daisy wouldn't leave me," he said, after a moment. "She could never love anybody but me."

She was listening and Gatsby saw that she was; he blinked continually now, as if the world were slipping sideways before his eyes.

To my surprise Tom began to talk with husky tenderness about their honeymoon, while from the ballroom below muffled and suffocating chords drifted in on hot waves of air.

"Do you remember how we used to swim in the early morning at Kapiolani, Daisy?"

"Please don't." All the rancor and scorn was gone from her voice. Her hand as she lit a cigarette was trembling.

"And the day I carried you all the way down from the Punch Bowl in my arms because you wanted to keep your shoes out of the rain——"

"I want to speak to you alone, Daisy," interrupted Gatsby quickly. "You're all excited——"

The sudden panic which made him willing to take her on her own terms, to run off with her tonight, was visible in his face. He was telling her that with every word and she knew it. But her courage was gone.

"You want too much," she said in a pitiful voice. "I can't say I never loved Tom. It wouldn't be true."

"Why there are things between Daisy and me that you'll never know," said Tom, "things that neither of us will forget."

Gatsby kept looking at Daisy.

"I don't ask you to say anything. I only want *you*, Daisy." She didn't answer and he turned miserably to Tom. "She never loved you. I have a way—I have reasons for knowing she never loved you. Good reasons. She only married you because you were rich and she was tired."

Those tragic eyes of Gatsby's were the criterion of Tom's triumph but the dead dream fought on while the afternoon slipped away, striving to touch what was no longer tangible, struggling unhappily, undespairingly, toward that lost voice across the room.

"She's never stopped loving me," said Tom and his words seemed to lean down over Gatsby. "Certainly not for a common swindler who'd have to steal the ring he put on her finger."

But Gatsby was too stunned to hear or care and Tom, who wasn't a bully except when he was drunk, saw that he had gone far enough. He could be magnanimous, and a little contemptuous now——

"It's pretty late. You two start on home"—he indicated his wife and Gatsby— "in the circus—in Mr. Gatsby's car. You wanted to talk to her and here's your chance. But I think you understand now that you're talking to my wife."

They were gone, with scarcely a word, with Daisy's inattributable tears. After a moment Tom got up and began wrapping the unopened bottle of whiskey in a towel.

"Want any of this stuff? Nick? . . . Jordan?"

"No thanks."

He looked at me, a little wistfully.

"Mr. Gatsby seemed unhappy," he remarked.

"What's that?"

"Weren't you listening?"

"I just remembered this is my birthday."

I was thirty. Before me stretched the portentous menacing road of a new decade.

It was seven o'clock by my watch when we got into the coupé with him and started for Long Island. Tom talked incessantly, boasting and laughing, but his voice was as remote as the voices of children on the sidewalk or the tumult of the elevated overheard. Jordan and I were driving out into the fresh country together and their tragic arguments were fading with the city lights behind. Thirty—a decade of loneliness, a thinning list of single men to know, a thinning assortment of illusions, thinning hair. As we passed over the dark, silky bridge all that remained to be said between Jordan and me was said in a whisper and the pressure of a hand.

So we drove on toward death through the cooling twilight.

The young Greek, Michaelis, who ran the coffee joint beside the ash-heaps was the principal witness at the inquest. He had slept through the heat, until after five, when he strolled over to the garage and found George Wilson sick in his office—really sick, pale as paste and shaking all over. Michaelis advised him to go to bed but Wilson refused, saying that he'd miss a lot of business if he did. While his neighbor was trying to persuade him a violent racket broke out overhead.

"I've got my wife locked in up there," explained Wilson calmly. "She's going to stay there till the day after tomorrow and then we're going to move away."

Michaelis was astonished; they had been neighbors for four years and Wilson had never seemed faintly capable of such a statement. Generally he was one of these wornout men: when he wasn't working he sat on a chair in the doorway and stared at the people and the cars that passed along the road. When anyone spoke to him he invariably laughed in an agreeable, colorless way. He was his wife's man and not his own.

So naturally Michaelis tried to find out what had happened, but Wilson wouldn't say a word—instead he began to throw curious, suspicious glances at his visitor and ask him what he'd been doing at certain times on certain days. Just as the latter was getting uneasy some workmen came past the door bound for his restaurant and he took the opportunity to get away, intending to come back later. But he never did. He didn't know why he didn't, he supposed he forgot it, that's all. When he came outside again a little after seven he was reminded of it because he heard Mrs. Wilson's voice, loud and scolding, downstairs in the garage.

"Beat me!" he heard her cry. "Throw me down and beat me, you dirty little coward!"

A moment later he saw her rush out into the dusk, waving her hands and shouting; before he could move from his door the business was over.

The "death car," as the newspapers called it, didn't stop; it came out of the gathering darkness, wavered tragically for a moment and then disappeared around the next bend. Michaelis wasn't even sure of its color—he told the first policeman that it was light green. The other car, the one going toward New York, came to rest a hundred yards beyond, and the driver hurried back to where Myrtle Wilson, her life violently extinguished, knelt in the road and mingled her thick, dark blood with the dust.

Michaelis and this man reached her first but when they had torn open her shirtwaist still damp with perspiration they saw that her left breast was swinging loose like a flap and there was no need to listen for the heart beneath. The mouth was wide open and ripped a little at the corners as though she had choked a little in giving up the tremendous vitality she had stored so long.

We saw the three or four automobiles and the crowd when we were still some distance away.

"Wreck!" said Tom. "That's good. Wilson'll have a little business at last."

He slowed down, but still without any intention of stopping until, as we came nearer, the hushed intent faces of the people at the garage door made him half unconsciously put on the brakes.

"We'll take a look," he said doubtfully, "just a look."

I became aware now of a gasping, moaning sound which issued incessantly from the garage, a sound which as we got out of the coupé and walked toward the door resolved itself into a hollow wail of "Oh, my God!" uttered over and over.

"There's some bad trouble here," said Tom excitedly.

He reached up on tiptoes and peered over a circle of heads into the garage, which was lit only by a yellow light in a swinging metal basket overhead. Then he made a harsh husky sound in his throat and with a violent, thrusting movement of his powerful arms pushed his way through.

The circle closed up again and there was a running murmur of expostulation; it was a minute before I could see anything at all. Then new arrivals disarranged the line, and Jordan and I were pushed suddenly inside.

Myrtle Wilson's body, wrapped in a blanket and then in another blanket as though she suffered from a chill in the hot night, lay on a work table by the wall and Tom, with his back to us, was bending over it, motionless. Next to him stood a motorcycle policeman taking down names with much sweat and correction in a little book. At first I couldn't find the source of the high, groaning words that echoed clamorously through the bare garage—then I saw Wilson standing on the raised threshold of his office, swaying back and forth and holding to the doorposts with both hands. Some man was talking to him in a low voice and attempting from time to time to lay a hand on his shoulder, but Wilson neither heard nor saw. His eyes would drop slowly from the swinging light to the laden table by the wall and then jerk back to the light again and he gave out incessantly his high horrible call:

"O my Ga-od! O my Ga-od! O Ga-od! O my Ga-od!"

Presently Tom lifted his head with a jerk and after staring around the garage with glazed eyes addressed a mumbled incoherent remark to the policeman.

"M-a-v—" the policeman was saying, "—o—"

"No, —r—" corrected the man, "M-a-v-r-o—"

"Listen to me!" muttered Tom fiercely.

"R–" said the policeman, "o—"

"G—"

"G—" He looked up as Tom's broad hand fell sharply on his shoulder. "What you want, fella?"

"What happened?—that's what I want to know."

"Auto hit her. In'santly killed."

"Instantly killed," repeated Tom, staring.

"She ran out ina road. Son of a bitch didn't even stop'z car."

"There was two cars," said Michaelis. "One comin', one goin', see?"

"Going where?" asked the policeman keenly.

"One goin' each way. Well, she—" his hand rose toward the blankets but stopped halfway and fell to his side, "—she ran out there an' the one comin' from N'York knock right into her goin' thirty or forty miles an hour."

"What's the name of this place here?" demanded the officer.

"Hasn't got any name."

A pale well dressed negro stepped near.

"It was a yellow car," he said. "Big yellow car. New."

"See the accident?" asked the policeman.

"No, but the car passed me down the road, going faster'n forty. Going fifty, sixty."

"Come here and let's have your name. Look out now. I want to get his name."

Some words of this conversation must have reached Wilson swaying in the office door for suddenly a new theme found voice among his gasping cries.

"You don't have to tell me what kind of car it was! I know what kind of car it was!"

Watching Tom I saw the wad of muscle back of his shoulder tighten under his coat. He walked quickly over to Wilson and standing in front of him seized him firmly by the upper arms.

"You've got to pull yourself together," he said with soothing gruffness.

Wilson's eyes fell upon Tom; he started up on his tiptoes and then would have collapsed to his knees had not Tom held him upright.

"Listen," said Tom, shaking him a little, "I just got here a minute ago, from New York. I was bringing you that coupé we've been talking about. That yellow car I was driving this afternoon wasn't mine, do you hear? I haven't seen it all afternoon."

Only the negro and I were near enough to hear what he said but the policeman caught something in the tone and looked over with truculent eyes.

"What's all that?" he demanded.

"I'm a friend of his." Tom turned his head but kept his hands firm on Wilson's body. "He says he knows the car that did it. . . . It was a yellow car."

Some dim impulse moved the policeman to look suspiciously at Tom.

"And what color's your car?"

"It's a blue car, a coupé."

"We've come straight from New York," I said.

Someone who had been driving a little behind us confirmed this and the policeman turned away.

"Now if you'll let me have that name again correct——"

Picking up Wilson like a doll Tom carried him into the office, set him down in a chair and came back.

"If somebody'll come here and sit with him!" he snapped authoritatively. He watched while two men standing closest glanced at each other unwillingly and went into the room. Then Tom shut the door on them and came down the single step, his eyes avoiding the table. As he passed close to me he whispered, "Let's get out."

Self consciously, with his authoritative arms breaking the way, we pushed through the still gathering crowd, passing a hurried doctor, case in hand, who had been sent for in wild hope half an hour ago.

Tom drove slowly until we were beyond the bend—then his foot came down hard and the coupé raced along through the night. In a little while I heard a low husky sob and saw that the tears were overflowing down his face.

"The God Damn coward!" he said. "He didn't even stop his car."

The Buchanan house floated suddenly toward us through the dark, rustling trees. Tom stopped beside the porch and looked up at the second floor where two windows bloomed with light among the vines.

"Daisy's home," he remarked. As we got out of the car he glanced at me and frowned slightly.

"I ought to have dropped you in West Egg, Nick. There's nothing we can do tonight."

A change had come over him and he spoke gravely, and with decision. As we walked across the moonlit gravel to the porch he disposed of the situation in a few brisk phrases.

"I'll telephone for a taxi to take you home. And while you're waiting you and Jordan better go in the kitchen and have them get you some supper—if you want any."

He opened the door.

"Come in."

"No thanks. But I'd be glad if you'd order me the taxi. I'll wait outside."

Jordan put her hand on my arm.

"Won't you come in, Nick?"

"No thanks."

I was feeling a little sick and I wanted to be alone. But Jordan lingered for a moment more.

"It's only half past nine," she said.

I'd be damned if I'd go in; I'd had enough of all of them for one day and suddenly that included Jordan too. She must have seen something of this in my expression for she turned away suddenly and ran up the porch steps into the house. I sat down for a few minutes with my head in my hands, until I heard the phone taken up inside and the butler's voice calling a taxi. Then I walked slowly down the drive away from the house intending to wait by the gate.

I hadn't gone twenty yards when I heard my name and Gatsby stepped from between two bushes into the path. I must have felt pretty weird by that time because I could think of nothing except the luminosity of his pink suit under the moon.

"What are you doing?" I inquired.

"Just standing here, old sport."

Somehow that seemed a despicable occupation. For all I knew he was going to rob the house in a moment; I wouldn't have been surprised to see sinister faces, the faces of "Wolfshiem's people," behind him in the dark shrubbery.

"Did you see any trouble on the road?" he asked after a minute.

"Yes."

He hesitated.

"Was she killed?"

"Yes."

"I thought so. I told Daisy I thought so. It's better that the shock should all come at once. She stood it pretty well."

He spoke as if Daisy's reaction was the only thing that mattered.

"I got to West Egg by a side road," he went on, "and left the car in my garage. I don't think anybody saw us but of course I can't be sure."

I disliked him so much by this time that I didn't find it necessary to tell him he was wrong.

"Who was the woman?" he inquired.

"Her name was Wilson. Her husband owns the garage."

"It was very hard luck," he said thoughtfully.

"What was the matter?" I demanded. "How'd you happen to hit her?"

"Well, I tried to swing the wheel——" He broke off, and suddenly I guessed at the truth.

"Was Daisy driving?"

"Yes," he said after a moment, "but of course I'll say I was. You see, when we left New York she was nervous and she thought it would calm her down if she drove, and it did for awhile, until just as we passed a car coming the other way this woman rushed out at us. It was all very quick but I got the impression that she wanted to speak to us, she thought we were somebody she knew. Well, Daisy isn't a very good driver and she did the instinctive thing, turned away from the woman toward the other car, and lost her nerve and turned back. The minute my hand reached the wheel I felt the shock—it must have killed her instantly."

"It ripped her open——"

"Don't tell me, old sport." He winced. "Anyhow—Daisy stepped on it. I tried to make her stop but she couldn't, and didn't until I pulled on the emergency brake. Then she collapsed into my lap. So I drove on."

"She'll be all right tomorrow," he said presently. "I'm just going to wait here and see if he tries to bother her about that row this afternoon. She's locked herself into her room and if he tries any brutality she's going to turn the light out and on again."

"He won't touch her," I said. "He's not thinking about her."

"I don't trust him."

"How long are you going to wait?"

"All night if necessary. Anyhow till they all go to bed."

He hadn't said a word about going away with Daisy, but I gathered he hadn't wanted her to come home at all. And another point of view occurred to me. Suppose Tom found out that Daisy had been driving. He might think he saw a connection in it—he might think anything. I looked at the house: there were two or three bright windows downstairs and the pink glow from Daisy's room on the second floor.

"You wait here," I said. "I'll see if there's any sign of a commotion."

I walked back along the border of the lawn, traversed the gravel softly and tiptoed up the veranda steps. The drawing room blinds were up and I saw that the room was empty. Crossing the porch where we had dined that June night three months before I came to a small rectangle of light which I guessed was the pantry window. The curtain was drawn but I found a rift at the sill.

Daisy and Tom were sitting opposite each other at the kitchen table with a plate of cold fried chicken between them and two bottles of ale. He was talking intently across the table at her and in his earnestness his hand had fallen upon and covered her own. Once in awhile she looked up at him and nodded in agreement.

They weren't happy, and neither of them had touched the chicken or the ale—and yet they weren't unhappy either. There was an unmistakable air of natural intimacy about the picture and anybody would have said that they were conspiring together.

As I tiptoed from the porch I heard my taxi feeling its way along the dark road toward the house. Gatsby was waiting where I had left him in the drive.

"Is it all right up there?" he asked anxiously.

"Yes, it's all right." I hesitated. "You'd better come home and get some sleep."

He shook his head.

"I want to wait here until Daisy goes to bed. Good night, old sport."

He put his hands in his coat pockets and turned back eagerly to his scrutiny of the house, as though my presence marred the sacredness of his vigil. So I walked away and left him standing there in the moonlight, watching over nothing.

CHAPTER VIII

I couldn't sleep all night; a fog-horn was groaning incessantly on the Sound, and I tossed half sick between grotesque reality and savage frightening dreams. Toward dawn I heard a taxi go up Gatsby's drive and immediately I jumped out of bed and began to dress—I felt that I had something to tell him, something to warn him about and morning would be too late.

Crossing his lawn I saw that his front door was still open and he was leaning against a table in the hall, heavy with dejection or sleep.

"Nothing happened," he said wanly. "I waited, and about four o'clock she came to the window and stood there for a minute and then turned out the light."

His house had never seemed so enormous to me as it did that night when we hunted through the great rooms for cigarettes. We pushed aside curtains that were like pavilions and felt over innumerable feet of dark wall for electric light switches—once I tumbled with a sort of splash upon the keys of a ghostly piano. There was an inexplicable amount of dust everywhere and the rooms were musty as though they hadn't been aired for many days. We found the humidor on an unfamiliar table with two stale dry cigarettes inside. Throwing open the French windows of the drawing room we sat smoking out into the darkness.

"You ought to go away," I said. "It's pretty certain they'll trace your car."

"Go away *now*, old sport?"

"Go to Atlantic City for a week, or up to Montreal."

He wouldn't consider it. He couldn't possibly leave Daisy until he knew what she was going to do. I might have told him, but if he was clutching at some last hope I couldn't bear to shake him free.

"You know, old sport, I haven't got anything," he said suddenly. "I thought for awhile I had a lot of things, but the truth is I'm empty, and I guess people feel it. That must be why they keep on making up things about me, so I won't be so empty. I even make up things myself." He looked at me frankly. "I'm not an Oxford man."

"I know it." I was glad that this tremendous detail was cleared up at last.

"I was only there a few months," he continued unexpectedly. "A lot of the officers overseas had a chance to go there after the war."

I wanted to slap him on the back. I had one of those renewals of complete faith in him that I had experienced before.

"I'll tell you everything," he broke out exuberantly. "The whole story. I've never told it to anyone before—not even Daisy. But I haven't told many lies about it, either, only I've shifted things around a good deal to make people wonder."

It was true, for example, that he had inherited money—but not from his parents, who were very needy and obscure, so much so that he had never really believed that they were his parents at all.

This sounds like a shoddy admission on his part but it wasn't. I understood what he meant—the fact that he was born in indisputable wedlock had never convinced his imagination and what better right does a man possess than to invent his own antecedents? Jay Gatsby of West Egg, Long Island, sprang from his platonic conception of himself. He was a son of God—a phrase which, if it means anything at all, means just that. And he must be about his Father's business, which was the service of a vast, vulgar and meretricious beauty. To this he was faithful till the end.

The part of his life he told me about began when he was fifteen, when the popular songs of those days began to assume for him a melancholy and romantic beauty. He attached them to reveries as transitory as themselves and attributed deep significance to melodies and phrases set down cynically in Tin-Pan Alley. For awhile these reveries provided an outlet for his imagination, reflecting with their contemporary glamour the gaudy universe in which he believed. They were a satisfactory hint of the unreality of reality, a promise that the rock of the world was founded securely on a fairy's wing.

At sixteen, James Gatz—that was really, or at least legally, his name—was beating his way along the south shore of Lake Superior as a clam digger and a salmon fisher or in any other capacity that brought him food and bed. His brown hardening body lived naturally through the half fierce, half lazy work of the bracing days. He knew women early and as they spoiled him he became contemptuous of them, of young virgins because they were ignorant, of the others because they were hysterical about things which in his overwhelming self absorption he took for granted.

But his heart was in a constant turbulent riot. The most grotesque and fantastic conceits haunted him in his bed at night. Plans affecting the destinies of great nations and gorgeous cities spun themselves out in his brain while the clock ticked on the washstand and the moon soaked with wet light his tangled clothes upon the floor. Each night he added to the pattern of his fancies until drowsiness closed down upon some vivid scene with an oblivious embrace.

An instinct toward his future glory led him once when he was seventeen to the small Lutheran college of St. Olaf's in northern Minnesota. He stayed there two weeks, dismayed at its ferocious indifference to the drums of his destiny, to destiny itself, and despising the janitor's work with which he was to pay his way through. Then he went back to Lake Superior intending to find regular employment and save enough to go east. He was still searching for something to do on the day that Dan Cody's yacht dropped anchor in the shallows along shore.

Cody was fifty years old then, a product of the Nevada silver fields, of the Yukon, of every rush for metal since seventy-five. The transactions in Montana copper that made him many times a millionaire found him physically robust but on the verge of soft-mindedness, and suspecting this an indefinite number of women tried to separate him from his money. The none too savory ramifications by which Ella Kaye, the newspaper woman, played Madame de Maintenon to his weakness and sent him to sea in a yacht were common property of the gaudy journalism of 1902. He had been coasting along all too hospitable shores for five years when he turned up as James Gatz's destiny in Little Girl Bay.

"I was loafing around the beach that morning, and I watched his boat come in to get water. I thought it was the prettiest thing I'd ever seen in my life, that boat, and I'd have given my shirt to go on board. Then I saw it was going to drop anchor over one of the worst flats along the shore—and the tide would be going out in a quarter of an hour. I borrowed a rowboat and pulled for the yacht, and told Dan Cody that he'd be broken up sure before noon. I had a hard time convincing him, but when I did he gave me ten silver dollars and invited me to lunch. He asked me my name and I told him it was Jay Gatsby—I had changed it the night before. He liked me and I liked him, so a couple of days later he took me to Duluth and bought me a blue coat and six pair of white duck trousers and a yachting cap. And when the "Tuolomee" left for the West Indies and the Barbary Coast I left too."

He was employed in a vague personal capacity—while he stayed with Cody he was in turn secretary, steward, mate, skipper and even jailor, for Dan Cody sober knew what lavish doings Dan Cody drunk might soon be about and he provided for such contingencies by reposing more and more trust in Gatsby. The arrangement lasted five years during which the boat went three times around the continent. It might have lasted indefinitely except for the fact that Ella Kaye came on board one night in Boston and a week later Dan Cody inhospitably died.

I remembered the portrait of him in Gatsby's bedroom, a grey florid man with a hard empty face—the pioneer debauchée who during one phase of American life brought back to the eastern seaboard the savage violence of the frontier brothel and saloon. I said as much and Gatsby nodded.

"That's why I never drink much. Somebody had to run things so I got into the habit of letting booze alone. I had a long sober look at the others—sometimes the women used to rub champagne in my hair."

"I suppose it was from him that you inherited money."

"Twenty-five thousand. But I never got it. I was young then and I still don't know exactly how they cheated me, old sport, but Ella Kaye got it all.

"That was in the spring of nineteen-thirteen," he continued after a moment. "I didn't have any luck for awhile after that."

He frowned and obliterating five years with a vague gesture began to talk about the war.

"I was glad when the war came. For one thing I was dead broke. I got into the first officers' camp, and they gave me a commission as first lieutenant. I enjoyed it, old sport, especially in the early morning, when we lined up for roll-call and you could still see the stars. I felt exhilarated like a kid again. I felt as if I could do anything—as if something absolutely wonderful was going to happen."

At first like so many young men of those days he thought he would stay in the army permanently. He was serenely happy—the effort was so austere, the goal so definite and attainable. Then he was sent to a cantonment near Louisville where one night he went with some other officers to a country club dance. Within a week his exhilaration quickened to a new note, the dark lovely voice of Daisy Fay.

She was the first "nice" girl he had ever known. In various unrevealed capacities he had come in contact with such people but always with indiscernible barbed-wire between. He found her excitingly desirable. He went to her house, at first with other officers, then alone. He was amazed at it—he had never been in such a beautiful house before. But what gave it an air of breathless intensity was that Daisy lived there—it was as casual a thing to her as was his tent out at camp to him. There was a ripe mystery about it, a hint of bedrooms upstairs more beautiful and cool than other bedrooms, of gay and radiant activities taking place through its corridors and of romances that were not musty and laid away already in lavender but fresh and breathing and redolent of this year's shining motorcars and of dances whose flowers were scarcely withered. It excited him too that many men had already loved Daisy—it increased her value in his eyes. He felt their presence all about the house, pervading the air with the shades and echoes of still vibrant emotions.

But he knew that he was in Daisy's house by a colossal accident. He knew that he was a nobody with an irrevealable past and that at any moment the invisible cloak of his uniform might slip from his shoulders. So he made the most of his time. He took what he could get, ravenously and unscrupulously—eventually he took Daisy one still October night, took her because he had no real right to touch her hand.

He might have despised himself, for he had certainly taken her under false pretenses. I don't mean that in this case he had claimed to be the son of a millionaire, but he had deliberately given Daisy a sense of security; he let her believe that he was a person from much the same strata as herself—that he was fully able to take care of her. As a matter of fact he had no such facilities—he had no comfortable family standing behind him and he was liable at the whim of an impersonal government to be blown anywhere about the world.

But he didn't despise himself—it didn't turn out as he had imagined. He had intended, probably, to take what he could and go—but now he found that he had committed himself to the following of a grail. He knew that Daisy was extraordinary but he didn't realize just how extraordinary a "nice" girl could be. She vanished into her rich house, into her rich, full life, leaving Gatsby—nothing. He felt married to her, that was all.

When they met again two days later it was Gatsby who was breathless, who was somehow betrayed. Her porch was bright with the bought luxury of star-shine; the wicker of the settee squeaked fashionably as she turned toward him and he kissed her curious and lovely mouth. She had caught a cold and made her voice huskier and more charming than ever and Gatsby was over-whelmingly aware only of the youth and mystery that wealth imprisons and preserves, of the freshness of many clothes and of Daisy, gleaming like silver, safe and proud above the hot struggles of the poor.

"I can't describe to you how surprised I was to find out I loved her. I felt as if there'd been a trick played on me. I went and told her part of the truth, sort of hoping that she'd throw me over—but it didn't make any difference, because she was in love with me too. She seemed to think I knew a lot about life, and it was just because I knew different things from her. Then we took that walk together one night, and suddenly I decided that she was what my dreams had been about all along. That made it all right. I thought out my life over again with Daisy in it, trying to figure how we could marry and struggle along on so many dollars a month. I didn't want to be great any more because I wouldn't admit to myself that there could be anything better than having her. What was the use of doing great things if I could have a better time telling her what I was going to do, while I held her in my arms?"

On the last afternoon before he went abroad, he sat with Daisy in his lap for a long, silent time. It was a cold fall day with fire in the room and her cheeks flushed. Now and then she moved and he changed his arm a little and once he kissed her dark shining hair. The afternoon had made them tranquil for awhile as if to give them rest for whatever sadness the next day promised. They had never been closer in their month of love nor communicated more profoundly one with another, than when she brushed silent lips against his coat's shoulder or when he touched the end of her fingers, gently, as though she were asleep.

He did well in the war. He was a captain before he went to the front and after the Argonne battles he got his majority and the command of the divisional machine guns. He had an instinct for the business and in a long war he might have gone far. After the armistice he tried frantically to get home but some complication or misunderstanding sent him to Oxford instead. He was worried now—there was a quality of nervous despair in Daisy's letters. She didn't see why he couldn't come. She was feeling the pressure of the world outside and she wanted to see him and feel his presence beside her and be reassured that she was doing the right thing after all.

For Daisy was young and her artificial world was redolent of orchids and pleasant, cheerful snobbery and orchestras which set the rhythm of the year, summing up the sadness and suggestiveness of life in new tunes. All night the saxophones wailed the hopeless comment of the "Beale Street Blues" while a hundred pairs of golden and silver slippers shuffled the shining dust. At the grey tea hour there were always rooms that throbbed incessantly with this low sweet fever, while fresh faces drifted here and there like rose petals blown by the sad horns around the floor.

Through this twilight universe Daisy began to move again with the season; suddenly she was again keeping half a dozen dates a day with half a dozen men and drowsing asleep at dawn with the beads and chiffon of an evening dress tangled among dying orchids on the floor beside her bed. And all the time something within her was crying for a decision. She wanted her life shaped now, immediately—and the decision must be made by some force—of love, of money, of unquestionable practicality—that was close at hand.

That force took shape in the middle of spring with the arrival of Tom Buchanan. There was a wholesome bulkiness about his person and his position and Daisy was flattered. Doubtless there was a certain struggle and a certain relief. The letter reached Gatsby while he was still at Oxford.

It was dawn now on Long Island and we went about opening the rest of the windows downstairs, filling the house with grey-turning, gold-turning light. The ghostly shadow of a tree fell abruptly across the dew and birds began to sing a little among the blue leaves. There was a slow pleasant movement in the air, scarcely a wind, promising a cool lovely day.

"It was almost a year before I managed to beat it into my head that I couldn't have her," went on Gatsby quietly, "but I convinced myself at last. I used to be glad that I wasn't in society, old sport, because I never ran into anyone who knew her or was liable to mention her name."

Once he had to go to Louisville on business; he stayed there a week walking the streets where their footsteps had clicked together through the November night and revisiting the quiet, out-of-the-way places where they had driven in her white car. Just as Daisy's house had always seemed to him more mysterious and gay than other houses so his idea of the city itself, even though she was gone from it, was pervaded with a melancholy beauty.

He left feeling that if he had searched harder he might have found her—that he was leaving her behind. The Pullman car was hot. He went out to the open vestibule and sat down on the porter's folding chair and the station slid away and the backs of unfamiliar buildings moved by. Then out into the spring fields, where a yellow trolley raced them for a minute with people in it who might once have seen the pale magic of her face along the casual street.

The track curved and now it was going away from the sun which, as it sank lower, seemed to spread itself in benediction over the vanishing city where she had drawn her breath. He stretched out his hand desperately as if to snatch only a wisp of air, to save a fragment of the spot that she had made lovely for him. But it was all going by too fast now for his blurred eyes and he knew that he had lost that part of it, the freshest and the best, forever.

It was nine o'clock when we finished breakfast and went out on the porch. The night had made a sharp difference in the weather and there was an autumn flavor in the air. The gardener, the last one of Gastby's old servants, came to the foot of the steps.

"Shall I drain the pool today, Mr. Gatsby? Leaves'll start falling pretty soon and then there's always trouble with the pipes."

"Not now," Gatsby answered. "Not today. I want to go in for awhile this afternoon."

I looked at my watch and stood up.

"Twelve minutes to my train."

I didn't want to go to the city. I wasn't worth a decent stroke of work but it was more than that—I didn't want to leave Gatsby. I missed that train, and then another, before I could get myself away.

"I'll call you up," I said finally.

"Do, old sport."

"I'll call you about noon."

We walked slowly down the steps.

"I suppose Daisy'll call too." He looked at me anxiously as if he hoped I'd corroborate this.

"I suppose so."

"Well, goodbye."

We shook hands and I started away. Just before I reached the hedge I remembered something and turned around.

"They're a rotten crowd," I shouted, across the lawn. "You're worth the whole damn bunch put together."

I've always been glad I said that. It was the only compliment I ever gave him, because I disapproved of him from beginning to end. First he laughed politely, then he accepted it for what it was worth and looked at me for a moment with an almost radiant smile. His gorgeous pink rag of a suit made a bright spot of color against the white steps and I thought of the night when I first came to his ancestral home three months before. The lawn and drive had been crowded with the faces of those who guessed at his corruption—and he had stood on those steps, concealing his incorruptible dream, as he waved them goodbye.

I thanked him for his hospitality. We were always thanking him for that—I and the others.

"Goodbye," I called. "I enjoyed breakfast, Gatsby."

Up in the city I tried for awhile to list the quotations on an interminable amount of stock, then I fell asleep in my swivel chair. Just before noon the phone woke me and I started up with sweat breaking out on my forehead. It was Jordan Baker; she often called me up at this hour because the uncertainty of her own movements between hotels and clubs and private houses made it hard to find her any other way. Usually her voice came over the wire as something fresh and cool as if a divot from some green golf links had come sailing in at the office window but this morning it seemed harsh and dry.

"I've left Daisy's house," she said. "I'm at Hempstead and I'm going down to Southampton this afternoon."

Probably she had good reasons for leaving Daisy but the fact annoyed me and her next remark made me rigid.

"You weren't so nice to me last night."

"How could it have mattered then?"

Silence for a moment. Then—

"However—I want to see you."

"I want to see you too."

"Well, suppose I don't go to Southampton and come into town this afternoon?"

"No—I don't think this afternoon."

"Very well."

"It's impossible this afternoon. Various——"

We talked like that for awhile and then abruptly we weren't talking any longer. I don't know which of us hung up with a sharp click but I know I didn't care. I couldn't have talked to her across a teatable that day if I never talked to her again in this world.

I called Gatsby's house a few minutes later but the line was busy. I tried four times; finally an exasperated central told me the wire was being kept open for long distance from Detroit. Taking out my time-table I drew a small circle around the three-fifty train. Then I leaned back in my chair and tried to think. It was just noon.

When I passed the ashheaps on the train that morning I had crossed deliberately to the other side of the car. I supposed there'd be a curious crowd around there all day with little boys searching for dark spots in the dust and some garrulous man telling over and over what had happened until it became less and less real even to him and he could tell it no longer and Myrtle Wilson's tragic achievement was forgotten. Now I want to go back a little and tell what happened at the garage after we left there the night before.

They had difficulty in locating the sister, Catherine. She must have broken her rule against drinking that night for when she arrived she was stupid with liquor and unable to understand that the ambulance had already gone to Flushing. When they convinced her of this she immediately fainted as if that was the intolerable part of the affair. Someone kind or curious took her in his car and drove her in the wake of her sister's body.

Until long after midnight a changing crowd lapped up against the front of the garage while George Wilson rocked himself back and forth on the couch inside. For awhile the door of the office was open and everyone who came into the garage glanced irresistibly through it. Finally someone said it was a shame and closed the door. Michaelis and several other men were with him—first four or five men, later two or three men. Still later Michaelis had to ask the last stranger to wait there fifteen minutes longer while he went back to his own place and made a pot of coffee. After that he stayed there alone with Wilson until dawn.

About three o'clock the quality of Wilson's incoherent muttering changed—he grew quieter and began to talk about the yellow car. He announced that he had a way of finding out who the yellow car belonged to, and then he blurted out that a month ago his wife had come from the city with her face bruised and a broken nose.

But when he heard himself say this he flinched and began to cry "Oh my God!" again in his groaning voice. Michaelis made a clumsy attempt to distract him.

"How long have you been married, George? Come on there, try and sit still a minute and answer my question. How long have you been married?"

"Twelve years."

"Ever had any children? Come on, George, sit still—I asked you a question. Did you ever have any children?"

The hard brown beetles kept thudding against the dull light and whenever Michaelis heard a car go tearing along the road outside it sounded to him like the car that hadn't stopped a few hours before. He didn't like to go into the garage because the work bench was stained where the body had been lying so he moved uncomfortably around the office—he knew every object in it before morning—and from time to time sat down beside Wilson trying to keep him more quiet.

"Have you got a church you go to sometimes, George? Maybe even if you haven't been there for a long time? Maybe I could call up the church and get a priest to come over and he could talk to you, see?"

"Don't belong to any."

"You ought to have a church, George, for times like this. You must have gone to church once. Didn't you get married in a church? Listen, George, listen to me. Didn't you get married in a church?"

"That was a long time ago."

The effort of answering broke the rhythm of his rocking—for a moment he was silent. Then the same half cunning, half bewildered look came back into his faded eyes.

"Look in the drawer there," he said, pointing at the desk.

"Which drawer?"

"That drawer—that one."

Michaelis opened the drawer nearest his hand. There was

nothing in it but a small expensive dog-leash made of leather and braided silver. It was apparently new.

"This?" he inquired, holding it up.

Wilson stared and nodded.

"I found it yesterday afternoon. She tried to tell me about it but I knew it was something funny."

"You mean your wife bought it?"

"She had it wrapped in tissue paper on her bureau."

Michaelis didn't see anything odd in that and he gave Wilson a dozen reasons why his wife might have bought the dog-leash. But possibly Wilson had heard some of these same explanations before, from Myrtle, because he began saying "Oh my God!" again in a whisper—his comforter left several explanations in the air.

"Then he killed her," said Wilson. His mouth dropped open suddenly.

"Who did?"

"I have a way of finding out."

"You're morbid, George," said his friend. "This has been a strain to you and you don't know what you're saying. You'd better try and sit quiet till morning."

"He murdered her."

"It was an accident, George."

Wilson shook his head. His eyes narrowed and his mouth widened slightly with the ghost of a superior "Hm!"

"I know," he said definitely. "I'm one of these trusting fellas and I don't think no harm to *no*body, but when I get to know a thing I know it. It was the man in that car. She ran out to speak to him and he wouldn't stop."

Michaelis had seen this too but it hadn't occurred to him that there was any special significance in it. He believed that Mrs. Wilson had been running away from her husband rather than trying to stop any particular car.

"How could she of been like that?"

"She's a deep one," said Wilson, as if that answered the question. "Ah-h-h——"

He began to rock again and Michaelis stood twisting the leash in his hand.

"Maybe you got some friend that I could telephone for, George?"

This was a forlorn hope—he was almost sure that Wilson had no friend: there was not enough of him for his wife. He was glad a little later when he noticed a change in the room, a blue quickening by the window, and realized that dawn wasn't far off. About five o'clock it was blue enough outside to snap off the light.

Wilson's glazed eyes turned to the ashheaps, where small grey clouds took on fantastic shape and scurried here and there in the faint dawn wind.

"I spoke to her," he muttered, after a long silence. "I told her she might fool me but she couldn't fool God. I took her to the window—" with an effort he got up and walked to the rear window and leaned with his face pressed against it, "—and I said 'God knows what you've been doing, everything you've been doing. You may fool me but you can't fool God!'"

Standing behind him Michaelis saw with a shock that he was looking at the eyes of Dr. T. J. Eckleburg which had just emerged pale and enormous from the dissolving night.

"God sees everything," repeated Wilson.

"That's an advertisement," Michaelis assured him. Something made him turn away from the window and look back into the room. But Wilson stood there a long time, his face close to the window pane, nodding into the twilight.

By six o'clock Michaelis was worn out and grateful for the sound of a car stopping outside. It was one of the watchers of the night before who had promised to come back so he cooked breakfast for three which he and the other man ate together. Wilson was quieter now and Michaelis went home to sleep. When he awoke four hours later and hurried back to the garage Wilson was gone.

His movements—he was on foot all the time—were afterwards traced to Port Roosevelt and then to Gad's Hill where he bought a sandwich that he didn't eat and a cup of coffee. He must have been tired and walking slowly for he didn't reach Gad's Hill until noon. Thus far there was no difficulty in accounting for his time—there were boys who had seen a man "acting sort of crazy" and motorists at whom he stared oddly from the side of the road. Then for three hours he disappeared from view. The police, on the strength of what he said to Michaelis, that he "had a way of finding out," supposed that he spent that time going from garage to garage thereabouts inquiring for a yellow car. On the other hand no garage man who had seen him ever came forward—and perhaps he had an easier, surer way of finding out what he wanted to know. By half-past two he was in West Egg where he asked someone the way to Gatsby's house. So by that time he knew Gatsby's name.

At two o'clock Gatsby put on his bathing suit and left word with the butler that if anyone phoned word was to be brought to him at the pool. He stopped at the garage for a pneumatic mattress that had amused his guests during the summer, and the chauffeur helped him pump it full of air. The chauffeur thought that he was "very nervous"; he'd given positive orders that the car wasn't to be taken out, and this seemed strange because the front right fender needed repair.

Gatsby shouldered the mattress and started for the pool. Once he stopped and shifted it a little and the chauffeur asked him if he needed help, but he shook his head and in a moment disappeared among the yellowing trees.

No telephone message arrived but the butler went without his sleep and waited for it until four o'clock—until long after there was anyone to give it to if it came. I have an idea that Gatsby himself didn't believe it would come and perhaps he no longer cared. If that was true he must have felt that he had lost the old warm world, paid a high price for living too long with a single dream. He must have looked up at an unfamiliar sky through frightening leaves and shivered as he found what a grotesque thing a rose is and how raw the sunlight was upon the scarcely created grass. A new world, material without being real, where poor ghosts, breathing dreams like air, drifted fortuitously about . . . like that ashen, fantastic figure gliding toward him through the amorphous trees.

The chauffeur, one of Wolfshiem's protegées, heard the shots— afterward he could only say that he hadn't thought anything much about them. I drove from the station directly to Gatsby's house and my rushing anxiously up the front steps was the first thing that alarmed anyone. But they knew then, I firmly believe. With scarcely a word said, four of us, the chauffeur, butler, gardener and I, hurried down to the pool.

There was a faint, scarcely perceptible movement of the water as the fresh flow from one end urged its way toward the drain at the other. With little ripples that were hardly the shadows of waves, the laden mattress moved irregularly down the pool. A small gust of wind that scarcely corrugated the surface was enough to disturb its accidental course with its accidental burden. The touch of a cluster of leaves revolved it slowly, tracing like the leg of a compass, a thin red circle in the water.

It was after we started with Gatsby toward the house that the gardener saw Wilson's body a little way off in the grass, and the holocaust was complete.

CHAPTER IX

After two years I remember the rest of that day, and that night and the next day, only as an endless drill of police and photographers and newspaper men in and out of Gatsby's front door. A rope stretched across the main gate and a policeman by it kept out the curious, but little boys soon discovered that they could enter through my yard and there were always a few of them clustered open-mouthed about the pool. Someone with a positive manner, perhaps a detective, used the expression "mad man" as he bent over Wilson's body that afternoon, and the adventitious authority of his voice set the key for the newspaper reports next morning.

Most of those reports were a nightmare—grotesque, circumstantial, eager and untrue. When Michaelis's testimony at the inquest brought to light Wilson's suspicions of his wife I thought the whole tale would shortly be served up in racy pasquinade—but Catherine, who might have said anything, didn't say a word. She showed a surprising amount of character about it too—looked at the coroner with determined eyes under that corrected brow of hers and swore that her sister had never seen Gatsby, that her sister was completely happy with her husband, that her sister had been into no mischief whatever. She convinced herself of it and cried into her handkerchief as if the very suggestion was more than she could endure. So Wilson was reduced to a man "deranged by grief" in order that the case might remain in its simplest form. And it rested there.

But all this part of it seemed remote and unessential. I found myself on Gatsby's side, and alone. From the moment I telephoned news of the catastrophe to West Egg village, every surmise about him, and every practical question, was referred to me. At first I was surprised and confused; then as he lay in his house and didn't move or breathe or speak hour upon hour it grew upon me that I was responsible, because no one else was interested—interested, I mean, with that intense personal interest to which everyone has some vague right at the end.

I called up Daisy half an hour after we found him, called her instinctively and without hesitation. But she and Tom had gone away early that afternoon, and taken baggage with them.

"Left no address?"

"No."

"Say when they'd be back?"

"No."

"Any idea where they are? How I could reach them?"

"I don't know. Can't say."

I wanted to get somebody for him. I wanted to go into the room where he lay and reassure him: "I'll get somebody for you, Gatsby. Don't worry. Just trust me and I'll get somebody for you——"

Meyer Wolfshiem's name wasn't in the phone book. The butler gave me his office address on Broadway and I called information, but by the time I had the number it was long after five and no one answered the phone.

"Will you ring again?"

"I've rung them three times."

"It's very important."

"Sorry. I'm afraid no one's there."

I went back to the drawing room and thought for an instant that they were chance visitors, all these people who suddenly filled it. But though they drew back the sheet and looked at Gatsby with shocked eyes, his protest continued in my brain.

"Look here, old sport, you've got to get somebody for me. You've got to try hard. I can't go through this thing alone."

Somebody started to ask me questions but I broke away and going upstairs looked hastily through the unlocked parts of his desk—he'd never told me definitely that his parents were dead. But there was nothing—only the picture of Dan Cody, a token of forgotten violence staring down from the wall.

Next morning I sent the butler to New York with a letter to Wolfshiem which asked for information and urged him to come down on the next train. That request seemed superfluous when I wrote it. I was sure he'd start when he saw the newspapers just as I was sure there'd be a wire from Daisy before noon—but neither a wire nor Mr. Wolfshiem arrived; no one arrived, except more police and photographers and newspaper men. When the butler brought back Wolfshiem's answer I began to have a feeling of defiance, of scornful solidarity between Gatsby and me against them all.

Dear Mr. Carraway. This has been one of the most terrible shocks of my life to me I hardly can believe that it is true at all. Such a mad act as that man did should make us all think, I cannot come down now as I'm tied up in some very important affairs and cannot get mixed up in this thing now. If there is anything I can do a little later let me know in a letter by Edgar. I hardly know where I am when I hear about a thing like this and am completely prostrated.

Yours Truly

Meyer Wolfshiem

and then a hasty addendum beneath:

Let me know about the funeral, etc. do not know his family at all.

I think it was on the third day that a telegram signed Henry C. Gatz arrived from a town in Minnesota. It said only that the sender was leaving immediately and to postpone the funeral until he came.

He turned out to be Gatsby's father, a solemn old man very helpless and dismayed, bundled up in a long cheap ulster against the warm September day. His eyes leaked continuously with excitement and when I took the bag and umbrella from his hands he began to pull so incessantly at his sparse grey beard that I had difficulty in getting off his coat. He was on the point of collapse so I took him into the music room and made him sit down while I sent for something to eat. But he wouldn't eat and the glass of milk spilled from his trembling hand.

"I saw it in the Chicago newspaper," he said. "It was all in the Chicago newspaper; I started right away."

"I didn't know how to reach you."

His eyes, seeing nothing, moved ceaselessly about the room.

"It was a mad man," he said. "He must have been mad."

I hesitated whether to tell him the truth, that Gatsby hadn't even been driving the car, but I was afraid to excite him any more.

"Wouldn't you like some coffee," I urged, "or some kind of sandwich?"

"I don't want anything. I'm all right now, Mr.——"

"Carraway."

"Well, I'm all right now. Where have they got Jimmy?"

I took him into the drawing room where his son lay, and left him there. Some little boys had come up on the steps and were looking into the hall; when I told them who had arrived they went reluctantly away.

After a little while Mr. Gatz opened the door and came out, his mouth ajar, his face flushed slightly, his eyes leaking isolated and unpunctual tears. He had reached an age where death no longer has the quality of ghastly surprise, and when he looked around him now for the first time and saw the height and splendor of the hall and the great rooms opening out from it into other rooms, his grief began to be mixed with a certain pride.

I helped him to a bedroom upstairs and while he took off his coat and vest I reminded him that I had deferred all arrangements until he came.

"I didn't know what you'd want, Mr. Gatsby——"

"Gatz is my name."

"—Mr. Gatz. I thought you might want to take the body west."

He shook his head.

"Jimmy always liked it better down East. He rose up to his position in the East. Were you a friend of my boy's, Mr.——"

"We were close friends."

"He had a big future before him, you know. He was only a young man but he had a lot of brain power here."

He touched his head impressively and I nodded.

"If he'd of lived he'd of been a great man. A man like James J. Hill. He'd of helped build up the country."

"That's true," I said uncomfortably.

He fumbled at the embroidered coverlet, trying to take it from the bed, and lay down stiffly—instantly he was asleep.

When the phone rang that night I felt sure that it was Daisy at last. But it was a man's voice, rather frightened—he wanted to know who I was before he would give a name.

"This is Mr. Carraway."

"Oh—" He sounded relieved. "This is Klipspringer."

I was relieved too for that seemed to promise another friend at Gatsby's grave. I didn't want it to be in the papers and draw a sightseeing crowd so I'd been calling up a few people myself. They were hard to find.

"The funeral's tomorrow," I said. "Three o'clock here at the house. I wish you'd tell anybody who'd be interested."

"Oh, I will," he broke out hastily. "Of course I'm not likely to see anybody, but if I do."

His tone made me suspicious.

"Of course you'll be there yourself."

"Well, I'll certainly try. What I called up about is——"

"Wait a minute," I interrupted. "How about saying you'll come?"

"Well, the fact is—the truth of the matter is that I'm staying with some people up here in Greenwich and they rather expect me to be with them tomorrow. In fact there's a sort of picnic or something. Of course I'll do my very best to get away."

I ejaculated an unrestrained "Huh!" and he must have heard me for he went on nervously.

"What I called up about was a pair of shoes I left there. I wonder if it'd be too much trouble to have the butler send them on. You see they're tennis shoes and I'm sort of helpless without them. I can't play tennis or anything. My address is care of B. F.——"

I didn't hear the rest of the name because I hung up the receiver.

After that I felt a certain shame for Gatsby—one low dog to whom I telephoned implied that he had got what he deserved. However, that was my fault, for he was one of those who used to sneer most bitterly at Gatsby on the courage of Gatsby's liquor and I should have known better than to call him.

The morning of the funeral I went up to New York to see Meyer Wolfshiem; I couldn't reach him any other way. The door that I pushed open on the advice of an elevator boy was marked "The Swastika Holding Company" and at first there didn't seem to be anyone inside. But when I 'd called "hello" several times in vain an argument broke out behind a partition and presently a lovely

Jewess appeared at an interior door and scrutinized me with black hostile eyes.

"Nobody's in," she said. "Mr. Wolfshiem's gone to Chicago."

The first part of this was obviously untrue for someone had begun to whistle tunelessly inside.

"Please say that Mr. Carraway wants to see him."

"I can't get him back from Chicago, can I?"

At this moment a voice, unmistakably Wolfshiem's, called "Stella!" from the other side of the door.

"Leave your name on the desk," she said quickly. "I'll give it to him when he gets back."

"But I know he's there."

She took a step toward me and began to slide her hands indignantly up and down her hips.

"You young men think you can force your way in here any time," she scolded. "We're getting sickintired of it. When I say he's in Chicago he's in Chi*c*ago."

I mentioned Gatsby.

"Oh-h-" She looked at me over again. "Will you just—what was your name?"

She vanished. In a moment Meyer Wolfshiem stood in the doorway, his face very solemn, holding out both hands. He drew me into his office, remarking in a reverent voice that it was a sad time for all of us and offered me a cigar.

"My memory goes back to when first I met him," he said. "A young major just out of the army and covered over with medals he got in the war. He was so hard up he had to keep on wearing his uniform because he couldn't buy some regular clothes. First time I saw him was when he come into Winebrenner's poolroom at Forty-third Street and asked for a job. He hadn't eat anything for a couple of days. 'Come on have some lunch with me,' I sid. He ate more than four dollars' worth of food in half an hour."

"Did you start him in business?" I inquired.

"Start him! I made him."

"Oh."

Gatsby's life seemed to have had the same accidental quality as his death.

"I raised him up out of nothing, right out of the gutter. I saw right away he was a fine-appearing gentlemanly young man and when he told me he was an Oggsford I knew I could use him good. I got him to join up in the American Legion and he used to stand high there. Right off he did some work for a client of mine up to Albany. We were so thick like that in everything—" he held up two bulbous fingers "—always together."

I wondered if this partnership had included the World's Series transaction in 1919—and what else it included. I kept wondering until last winter, when Wolfshiem was tried (but not convicted) on ten charges ranging from simple bribery to dealing in stolen bonds.

"Now he's dead," I said after a moment. "You were his closest friend so I thought you ought to know his funeral is this afternoon."

"I'd like to come."

"Well, come then."

The hair in his nostrils quivered slightly and as he shook his head his eyes filled with tears.

"I can't do it—I can't get mixed up in it," he said.

"There's nothing to get mixed up in. It's all over now."

"When a man gets killed I never like to get mixed up in it in any way. I keep out. When I was a young man it was different—if a friend of mine died, no matter how, I stuck with them to the end. You may think that's sentimental but I mean it, to the bitter end."

I saw that for some reason of his own he was determined not to go to Gatsby's funeral so I stood up.

"Are you a college man?" he inquired suddenly.

For a moment I thought he was going to suggest a "gonnegtion" but he only nodded and shook my hand.

"Let us learn to show our friendship for a man when he is alive and not after he is dead," he suggested. "After that my own rule is to let everything alone."

When I left his office the sky had turned dark and I got back to West Egg in a drizzle. After changing my clothes I went next door and found Mr. Gatz walking up and down excitedly in the hall.

His pride in his son and in his son's possessions was continually increasing and now he had something to show me.

"My son sent me this picture." He took out his wallet with trembling fingers. "Look there."

It was a photograph of the house, cracked in the corners and dirty with many hands. He pointed out every detail to me eagerly. "Look there," and then sought admiration from my eyes. He had showed it so often that I think it was more real to him now than the house itself.

"Jimmy sent it to me. I think it's a very pretty picture. It shows up well."

"Very well. Had you seen Jimmy lately?"

"He came out to see me three years ago and bought me the house I live in now. Of course we was broke up when he run off from home but I see now there was a reason for it. He knew he had a big future in front of him. And ever since he made a success he was very generous with me."

He seemed reluctant to put away the picture, held it for another minute, lingeringly, before my eyes. Then he returned the wallet and pulled from his pocket a ragged old copy of a book called "Hopalong Cassidy."

"Look here. This is a book he had when he was a boy. It just shows you."

He opened it at the back cover and turned it around for me to see. On the last fly-leaf was printed the word SCHEDULE, heavily underlined, and the date September 12th, 1906. And underneath:

Get up 6.00	A.M.
Dumbbell exercise. . . . . 6.15—6.30	"
Study electricity, etc. . . . . 7.15—8.15	"
Work . . . . 8.30—4.30	P.M.
Baseball and sports . . . . 4.30—5.00	"
Practice elocution, poise and how to attain it . . . . 5.00—6.00	"
Study needed inventions . . . . 7.00—9.00	"

GENERAL RULES
No wasting time at Shafters or [a name, indecipherable].
No more smoking or chewing
Bath every other day

Read one improving book or magazine per week.
Save $5.oo [crossed out] $3.oo per week
Be better to parents.

"I came upon this book by accident," said the old man. "It just
shows you, don't it?"

"It just shows you."

"Jimmy was bound to get ahead. He always had some schedule
like this or something. Do you notice what he's got about improving his mind? He was always great for that. He told me I et like a
hog once, and I beat him for it."

He was reluctant to close the book, reading each item aloud and
then looking eagerly at me. I think he rather expected me to copy
down the list for my own use.

A little before three the Lutheran minister arrived from Flushing
and I began to look involuntarily out the windows for other cars.
So did Gatsby's father. And as the time passed and the servants
came in and stood waiting in the hall his eyes began to blink
anxiously and he spoke of the rain in a shocked worried way. The
minister glanced several times at his watch so I took him aside and
asked him to wait for half an hour. But it wasn't any use. Nobody
came.

About five o'clock our procession of three cars reached the
cemetery and stopped in a thick drizzle beside the gate—first a
motor hearse, horribly black and wet, then Mr. Gatz and the
minister and I in the limousine, and, a little later, four or five
servants and the postman from West Egg, piled into Gatsby's
station wagon and wet to the skin.

The undertaker, in a black oilskin raincoat, had hurried on
ahead. Now he came back and nodded to his assistants who slid
the casket out into the rain. As we started through the gate into the
cemetery I heard a car stop and then the sound of someone
splashing after us over the soggy ground. I looked around. It was
the man with owl-eyed glasses whom I had found marvelling over
Gatsby's books in the library one night three months before.

I'd never seen him since then. I don't know how he knew about the funeral or even his name. The rain poured down his thick glasses and he took them off and wiped them to see the protecting canvas unrolled from Gatsby's grave.

I tried to think about Gatsby then for a moment but he was already too far away and I could only remember with dull anger that Daisy hadn't sent a message or a flower. Dimly I heard someone murmur: "Blessed are the dead that the rain falls on," and then the owl-eyed man said "Amen to that" in a brave voice.

It was over. We straggled down quickly through the rain to the cars.

Owl-eyes spoke to me for a moment by the gate.

"I couldn't get to the house," he said.

"Neither could anybody else."

"Go on!" He started. "Why, my God! they used to go there by the hundreds."

He took off his glasses and wiped them again outside and in.

"The poor son-of-a-bitch," he said.

One of my most vivid memories is of coming back west from prep school and later from college at Christmas time. Those who went farther than Chicago would gather in the old dim La Salle Street Station at six o'clock of a November evening with a few Chicago friends already caught up into their own holiday gayeties to bid them a hasty goodbye. I remember the fur coats of the girls returning from Miss This or That's and the chatter of frozen breath and the hands waving overhead as we caught sight of old acquaintances and the matchings of invitations: "Are you going to the Ordways'? the Herseys'? the Schultzes'?" and the long green tickets clasped tight in our gloved hands. And last the murky yellow cars of the Chicago, Milwaukee & St. Paul railroad looking cheerful as Christmas itself on the tracks beside the gate.

When we pulled out into the winter night and the real snow, our snow, began to stretch out beside us and twinkle against the windows, and the dim lights of small Wisconsin stations moved by, a sharp wild brace came suddenly into the air. We drew in deep breaths of it as we walked back from dinner through the cold vestibules, unutterably aware of our identity with this country for one strange hour, before we melted indistinguishably into it again.

That's my middle-west—not the wheat or the prairies or the lost Swede towns but the thrilling, returning trains of my youth and the street lamps and sleigh bells in the frosty dark and the shadows of holly wreaths thrown by lighted windows on the snow. I am part of that, a little solemn with the feel of those long winters, a little complacent from growing up in the Carraway house in a city where dwellings are still called through decades by a family's name. I see now that this has been a story of the West, after all—Tom and Gatsby, Daisy and Jordan and I, were all Westeners, and perhaps we possessed some deficiency in common which made us subtly unadaptable to Eastern life.

Even when the East excited me most, even when I was most keenly aware of its superiority to the bored, sprawling, swollen towns beyond the Mississippi, with their interminable inquisitions which spared only the children and the very old—even then it had always for me a quality of distortion. West Egg especially still figures in my more fantastic dreams. I see it as a night scene by El Greco: a hundred houses, at once conventional and grotesque, crouching under a sullen, overhanging sky and a lustreless moon. In the foreground four solemn men in dress suits are walking along the sidewalk with a stretcher on which lies a drunken woman in a white evening dress. Her hand, which dangles over the side, sparkles cold with jewels. Gravely the men turn in at a house—the wrong house. But no one knows the woman's name, and no one cares.

After Gatsby's death the East was haunted for me like that, distorted beyond my eyes' power of correction. So when the blue smoke of brittle leaves was in the air and the wind blew the wet laundry stiff on the line I decided to come back home.

There was one thing to be done before I left, an awkward, unpleasant thing that perhaps had better have been let alone. But I wanted to leave things in order and not just trust that obliging and indifferent sea to sweep my refuse away. I saw Jordan Baker and talked over and around what had happened to us together and what had happened afterwards to me, and she lay perfectly still listening in a big chair.

She was dressed to play golf and I remember thinking she looked like a good illustration, her chin raised a little jauntily, her hair the color of an autumn leaf, her face the same brown tint as the fingerless glove on her knee. When I had finished she told me without comment that she was engaged to another man. I doubted that though there were several she could have married at a nod of her head but I pretended to be surprised. For just a minute I wondered if I wasn't making a mistake, then I thought it all over again quickly and got up to say goodbye.

"Nevertheless you did throw me over," said Jordan suddenly. "You threw me over on the telephone. I don't give a damn about you now but it was a new experience for me and I felt a little dizzy for awhile."

We shook hands.

"Oh, and do you remember—" she added "—a conversation we had once about driving a car?"

"Why—not exactly."

"You said a bad driver was only safe until she met another bad driver?"

For a moment I thought she was talking about Daisy's accident, but she wasn't.

"Well, I met another bad driver, didn't I? I mean it was careless of me to make such a bad guess. I thought you were rather an honest, straightforward person. I thought it was your—secret pride."

"I'm thirty," I said. "It's five years too late for me to lie to myself and call it honor."

She didn't answer. Angry and half in love with her, and tremendously sorry, I turned away.

One afternoon late in October I saw Tom Buchanan. He was walking ahead of me along Fifth Avenue in his alert, aggressive way, his hands out a little from his body as if to fight off interference, his head moving sharply here and there, adapting itself to his restless eyes. Just as I slowed up to avoid overtaking him he stopped abruptly and began frowning into the windows of a jewelry store. Then he saw me and walked back holding out his hand.

"What's the matter Nick? Do you object to shaking hands with me?"

"Yes—rather. You know what I think of you."

"You're crazy, Nick," he said quickly. "Crazy as hell. I don't know what's the matter with you."

"Tom," I inquired, "what did you say to Wilson that afternoon?"

He stared at me without a word and I knew I had guessed right about those missing hours. I started to turn away but he took a step after me and grabbed my arm.

"I told him the truth," he said quickly. "He came to the door while we were getting ready to leave and when I sent down word that we weren't in he tried to force his way upstairs. He was crazy enough to kill me if I hadn't told him who owned the car. His hand was on a revolver in his pocket every minute he was in the house——" He broke off defiantly. "What if I did tell him? That fellow had it coming to him. He threw dust into your eyes just like he did in Daisy's but he was a tough one. He ran over Myrtle like you'd run over a dog and never even stopped his car."

There was nothing I could say, except the one unutterable fact that it wasn't true.

"And if you think I didn't have my share of suffering—look here, when I went to give up that flat and saw that damn box of dog biscuits sitting there on the sideboard I sat down and cried like a baby. By God it was awful——"

I couldn't forgive him or like him but I saw that what he had done was, to him, utterly justified. It was all very careless and confused. They were careless people, Tom and Daisy—they smashed up things and people and then retreated back into their money or their vast carelessness or whatever it was that kept them together, and let other people clean up the mess they had made. . . .

I shook hands with him; it seemed silly not to, for I felt suddenly as though I were talking to a child. Then he went into the jewelry store to buy a pearl necklace or perhaps only a pair of cuff buttons, rid of my provincial squeamishness forever.

Gatsby's house was still empty when I left—the grass on his lawn had grown as long as mine. One of the taxi drivers in the village never took a fare past the entrance gate without stopping for a minute and pointing inside; perhaps it was he who drove Daisy and Gatsby over to East Egg the night of the accident and perhaps he had made a story about it all his own. I didn't want to hear it and I avoided him when I got off the train.

I spent my Saturday nights in New York because those gleaming, dazzling parties of his were with me so vividly that I could still hear the music and the laughter faint and incessant from his garden and the cars going up and down his drive. One night I did hear a material car there and saw its lights stop at his front steps. But I didn't investigate. Probably it was some last guest who had been away at the ends of the earth and didn't know that the party was over.

On the last night, with my trunk packed and my car sold to the grocer, I went over and looked at that huge incoherent failure of a house once more. On the white steps an obscene word, scrawled by some boy with a piece of brick, stood out clearly in the moonlight and I erased it, drawing my shoe raspingly along the stone. Then I wandered down to the beach and sprawled out on the sand.

Most of the big shore places were closed now and there were hardly any lights except the shadowy glow of a ferryboat across the Sound. And as the moon rose higher the inessential houses themselves began to melt away until gradually I became aware of the old island here that flowered once for Dutch sailors' eyes—a fresh, green breast of the new world. Its vanished trees, the trees that had made way for Gatsby's house, had once pandered in whispers to the last and greatest of all human dreams; for a transitory enchanted moment man must have held his breath in the presence of this continent, compelled into an aesthetic contemplation he neither understood nor desired, face to face for the last time in history with something commensurate to his capacity for wonder.

And as I sat there, brooding on the old unknown world, I thought of Gatsby's wonder when he first picked out the green light at the end of Daisy's dock. He had come a long way to this blue lawn and his dream must have seemed so close that he could hardly fail to grasp it. He did not know that it was already behind him, somewhere back in that vast obscurity beyond the city, where the dark fields of the republic rolled on under the night.

Gatsby believed in the green light, the orgastic future that year by year recedes before us. It eluded us then but never mind—tomorrow we will run faster, stretch out our arms farther. . . . And one fine morning——

So we beat on, boats against the current, borne back ceaselessly into the past.

RECORD OF VARIANTS

Substantives

The printed galley text is the base text. The holograph is the primary source for substantive emendations made in this galley text. Entries preceded by asterisks are readings corrected by Fitzgerald in the galleys. Readings marked *stet* are possible emendations (most of them involving colloquial speech) that have not been made. Notes give evidence that bears on the emendation decisions. The first reading in each entry is the reading printed in this edition of *Trimalchio*. It is followed by the rejected reading(s). Sigla give the sources of the readings and emendations. The following sigla and symbols are used:

FSF Fitzgerald
MS holograph of the novel
G printed text of Princeton galleys
A1 first printing of *Gatsby* (Scribners, 1925)
ed independent editorial emendation
^ space, or absence of punctuation or paragraphing
~ the same word

preliminaries The galleys contain no text for the preliminaries (half-title, list of books by FSF, title, copyright, and dedication pages). The title page of *The Great Gatsby* bears, as an epigraph, four lines of poetry by FSF, attributed to Thomas Parke D'Invilliers, a character in *This Side of Paradise*. The dedication page of the published novel reads "ONCE AGAIN | TO | ZELDA".

5.32 Gatsby who was] ed; Gatsby, the man who gives his name to this book, that was MS, G, A1
  See the introduction, p. xxii.
*9.16 walks] MS, A1; walls G
12.19 God Damn] MS; God damned G, A1
  Unaltered in G.
14.36 This idea] *stet*
  The MS reads "The idea".

16.20   at the table] *stet*
         The MS reads "at table".
*18.12   boots] MS, A1; books G
*21.17   Dr.] MS; Doctor G, A1
         FSF's "Dr." is consistent in MS and is retained throughout the
         text of *Trimalchio*.
*21.21   Queens] A1; Flushing MS, G
         A geographical correction by FSF in galleys. Flushing is a city,
         then chiefly residential, in the northern part of the borough of
         Queens.
*24.15   indeterminate] MS, A1; intermediate G
24.18   kind do you want] *stet*
         The MS reads "kind you want".
25.34   all] MS; all the G
*26.23   at a] MS, A1; at an G
*29.26   hated] MS, A1; hate G
30.23   They've been] *stet*
         The MS reads "They been".
32.24   lying] A1; lieing MS; being G
         FSF altered the typo "being" to the misspelled "lieing" in G.
*35.16   drunk] MS, A1; drink G
38.22   they all] ed; we all MS, G
         Because the entire passage containing these words was cut by
         FSF in G, no correction was made there. For Nick's comment to
         make sense, the reading must be "they all". The problem origi-
         nated in MS, where the passage is cast in the first person ("we ...
         we ... us"). FSF appears to have revised in a lost TS stage so that
         Nick excludes himself and Jordan from the crowd, but the initial
         change from "we" to "they" was not made.
*39.37   corners] MS, A1; corner G
42.34   formed with] MS; formed for G, A1
         Uncorrected in G.
46.32   little] MS, A1; a little G
         The "a" is deleted in G in an unknown hand.
53.16   running board] ed; dashboard MS, G, A1
*57.19   well-fanned] MS, A1; well-framed G
*58.37   your] MS, A1; you G
*62.33   a monkey] MS, A1; monkey G
*64.2   amour] MS, A1; an amour G
*64.15   voices] MS, A1; voice G

65.4　　a regular] MS; regular G, A1
　　　　Uncorrected in G.

*65.13　at his] A1; at her G
　　　　The sentence in which the reading appears is not present in MS. FSF corrected to "his" in G.

*68.1　　expanse] A1; expense G
　　　　FSF made the correction in G. In MS he left a blank space in the sentence, unable to call to mind the word he wanted.

*71.1　　November] A1; February MS, G
　　　　FSF corrected to "November" in G in order to make the month here match the month of Gatsby's departure from Louisville. See Chapter VIII, p. 123.

91.18　At his lips' touch] ed, A1; At his lips^ touch MS; As his lips touched G

*92.30　fans.] A1; fans. I always think of Daisy as lying on that couch with her dress fluttering. I never saw her after that day. MS, G
　　　　FSF cut the two sentences in G because Nick does in fact see Daisy once more – through the pantry window of her house.

94.14　preceded by] ed; preceeding MS; preceding G
　　　　FSF cut the sentence in G and so did not correct it there.

94.15　ice] MS; eyes G
　　　　FSF cut the sentence in G and so did not correct it there.

96.23　heads] *stet*
　　　　The MS reads "head".

97.3　　hot green] ed; orange MS, G; hot, green A1
　　　　FSF made the change (with no dividing comma) in G for internal consistency with "green leather conservatory" at 53.30.

98.6　　stop] MS; spot G, A1
　　　　Uncorrected in G.

98.30　I've been] *stet*
　　　　The MS reads "I been".

*100.21　times] A1; times in the next five squares MS, G
　　　　FSF made the correction in galleys. There were no squares in the street layout of New York City along the route that Tom and Gatsby were following to the Plaza.

109.6　Michaelis] ed; Mavromichaelis MS, G, A1
　　　　FSF changed the character's name to Michaelis between MS and G, but this one instance was missed and remained uncorrected into A1. With the change, the character spelling his name to the policeman later in the scene becomes a different person.

No confusion is created for the reader by revision or emendation.

110.2   disarranged] MS; deranged G, A1
          Uncorrected in G.
112.23   God Damn] MS; God damned G, A1
          Unaltered in G.
112.34   moonlit] MS; moonlight G, A1
          Uncorrected in G.
*114.30   he said] MS, A1; she said G
*122.31   tunes] MS, A1; times G
123.36   into] MS; in G, A1
          Uncorrected in G.
*124.33   shouted] MS, A1; shooted G
131.13   compass] ed; transept MS, G; transit A1
          Uncorrected in G but corrected at Scribners to "transit" before
          A1. In a 10 April 1924 letter Fitzgerald wrote Perkins: "Transit
          will do fine though of course I really meant compass."
134.16   addendum] ed; addenda MS, G, A1
          Uncorrected in G.
137.23   a reverent voice] A1; a reverend voice G; a whisper MS
          Uncorrected in G.

Space breaks

Space breaks are structurally important in the novel. They follow these
words in MS:

17.31   fool.
23.33   alive."
84.5   house.
107.18   wife."
119.22   died.
121.3   hand.
129.24   twilight.
130.9   name.
136.31   him.

No breaks appear at these points in the galleys, and breaks were not
restored by Fitzgerald at these junctures. He did restore breaks from the
MS after the following words in the galleys, and these breaks appear in the
text of *Trimalchio* published in this edition:

122.17   asleep.
123.13   Oxford.
145.2   forever.

Comma variants

Each word in the table below is followed by a comma in the galleys but by no punctuation in the MS. The MS readings have been adopted for the Cambridge text.

5.7 more; 5.8 way; 5.9 consequence; 5.17 preoccupation; 5.19 men; 5.20 them; 5.23 suggested; 5.28 marshes; 6.1 Gatsby; 6.17 clan; 6.19 brother; 6.20 War; 6.22 great-uncle; 6.28 world; 6.31 business; 6.33 me; 6.33 said; 6.33 ye-es; 6.34 year; 7.1 city; 7.2 season; 7.4 town; 7.7 Washington; 7.9 woman; 7.21 read; 7.21 thing; 7.23 securities; 8.5 story; 8.18 pool; 8.19 Or; 8.20 Gatsby; 8.22 eyesore; 8.23 lawn; 8.28 removed; 9.1 instance; 9.7 move; 9.8 heart; 9.9 seeking; 9.9 wistfully; 9.14 mansion; 9.29 lacing; 10.2 Society; 10.9 arm; 10.11 deep; 10.11 roses; 10.13 Demaine; 10.14 politely; 10.21 ceiling; 10.25 white; 10.31 room; 10.34 motionless; 10.35 little; 10.37 indeed; 11.8 witty; 11.16 rate; 11.17 imperceptibly; 11.22 cousin; 11.24 down; 11.29 gay; 11.33 east; 11.36 wreath; 12.7 Buchanan; 12.7 room; 12.18 me; 12.29 No; 12.35 Baker; 12.36 girl; 12.37 carriage; 13.11 mine; 13.14 hips; 13.15 porch; 13.16 sunset; 13.18 Daisy; 13.32 to; 13.33 great; 13.33 big; 13.34 Rain; 13.34 Baker; 13.37 great; 13.37 big; 14.11 West; 14.12 close; 14.16 remark; 14.22 book; 14.25 Daisy; 14.30 us; 14.30 race; 14.34 Baker; 14.36 am; 14.36 are; 14.36 are; 15.1 nod; 15.2 art; 15.4 concentration; 15.15 night; 15.18 worse; 15.23 regret; 15.25 ear; 15.25 chair; 15.28 table; 15.32 extemporizing; 15.32 her; 16.2 beyond; 16.4 excitedly; 16.22 boots; 16.23 me; 16.26 minute; 16.28 dinner; 16.33 everyone; 16.35 thinking; 16.35 Baker; 16.36 scepticism; 17.4 Baker; 17.4 them; 17.5 while; 17.6 deaf; 17.27 feeling; 18.6 face; 19.21 all; 19.31 people; 19.36 rumors; 20.5 Tom; 20.10 roofs; 20.14 night; 20.17 moonlight; 20.17 it; 20.22 himself; 21.3 mile; 21.7 smoke; 21.8 men; 21.13 cloud; 21.18 face; 21.21 Queens; 21.22 blindness; 21.26 and; 21.28 minute; 22.1 about; 22.3 afternoon; 22.4 and; 22.4 elbow; 22.7 luncheon; 22.11 fence; 22.15 it; 22.17 restaurant; 22.22 blind; 22.24 overhead; 22.26 anaemic; 22.28 Hello; 22.35 it; 23.2 stairs; 23.7 beauty; 23.9 and; 23.10 ghost; 23.11 lips; 23.14 Oh; 23.14 hurriedly; 24.1 muslin; 24.4 magazine; 24.5 Upstairs; 24.10 and; 24.10 forward; 24.16 eagerly; 24.33 somewhere; 24.34 lap; 25.3 pastoral; 25.16 purchases; 25.18 And;

25.18 course; 25.18 sister; 25.21 bedroom; 25.23 it; 25.26 distance; 25.26 however; 25.27 bonnet; 25.30 Peter; 25.32 milk; 25.33 large; 25.37 life; 26.1 dim; 26.2 it; 26.4 cigarettes; 26.6 disappeared; 26.8 things; 26.13 thirty; 26.14 solid; 26.14 hair; 26.16 angle; 26.20 haste; 26.23 aloud; 26.24 pale; 26.25 shaved; 26.25 cheekbone; 26.27 game; 26.30 handsome; 26.33 before; 26.35 chiffon; 27.3 moment; 27.4 her; 27.6 high; 27.8 feet; 27.21 Wilson; 27.23 side; 27.30 again; 28.2 ecstasy; 28.9 Gulls; 28.12 Island; 28.25 way; 28.27 Island; 28.29 Tom; 28.31 you; 28.32 asked; 29.8 Myrtle; 29.9 question; 29.12 Catholic; 29.13 Catholic; 29.24 started; 29.31 mistake; 29.34 Chester; 30.1 Myrtle; 30.7 breeding; 30.13 me; 30.27 sandwiches; 30.29 twilight; 30.30 wild; 30.36 mine; 31.4 shoes; 31.4 him; 31.6 me; 31.7 arm; 31.8 policeman; 31.10 about; 31.11 over; 31.17 wave; 31.17 dog; 31.18 trays; 31.27 smoke; 31.31 discussing; 31.31 voices; 31.35 movement; 31.37 floor; 32.7 couch; 32.7 fluently; 32.10 chandelier; 32.11 suggested; 32.25 Tribune; 33.6 raft; 33.12 servants; 33.12 gardener; 33.25 designs; 33.26 bar; 33.27 rail; 33.31 affair; 33.32 piccolos; 34.2 parked; 34.2 deep; 34.4 colors; 34.4 ways; 34.5 swing; 34.6 outside; 34.7 laughter; 34.8 introductions; 34.10 spot; 34.11 sun; 34.11 music; 34.13 prodigality; 34.17 group; 34.17 then; 34.18 triumph; 34.20 gypsies; 34.20 opal; 34.21 and; 34.22 Frisco; 34.23 her; 34.30 Island; 34.32 Gatsby; 35.4 times; 35.5 before; 35.6 Gatsby; 35.8 seven; 35.8 ill-at-ease; 35.8 hour; 35.10 host; 35.11 way; 35.12 movements; 35.29 dresses; 35.36 Jordan; 35.37 started; 36.1 woman; 36.14 low; 36.15 bankers; 36.16 bonds; 36.18 vicinity; 36.20 twilight; 36.20 produced; 36.21 doubt; 36.22 mine; 36.24 twilight; 36.29 girl; 36.32 Lucille; 37.18 us; 37.19 Oh; 37.30 served; 37.30 party; 37.33 innuendo; 38.12 God; 38.19 chair; 38.20 smile; 38.20 dark; 38.22 limbs; 38.23 limbs; 38.26 up; 38.29 crowded; 38.32 door; 38.32 library; 38.35 man; 38.35 spectacles; 39.11 fact; 39.13 granted; 39.17 stop; 39.19 shelf; 40.7 Italian; 40.7 jazz; 40.9 garden; 40.9 happy; 40.10 twins; 40.11 costume; 40.16 girl; 40.18 champagne; 40.20 elemental; 40.22 said; 40.28 vicinity; 40.29 hydro-plane; 41.11 person; 41.11 was; 41.12 somehow; 41.14 absurdity; 41.30 imperatively; 41.32 work; 41.37 condescension; 42.7 patronizingly; 42.11 proves; 42.11 told; 42.12 ages; 42.17 them; 42.21 cycle; 42.25 steps; 42.29 over; 42.32 groups; 42.33 Gatsby; 42.34 shoulder; 42.36 he; 43.6 side; 43.10 pardon; 43.20 long; 43.21 undergraduate; 43.23 girls; 43.25 piano; 43.25 tall; 43.27 champagne; 43.27 decided; 43.28 ineptly; 43.28 very; 43.28 very; 43.29 weeping; 43.30 gasping; 43.30 sobs; 43.33 deep; 43.35 face; 43.36 chair; 44.7 wife; 44.8 way; 44.10 diamond; 44.24 credibility; 44.24 struggle; 44.25 lifted; 44.25 kicking; 44.31 pale; 44.37

guests; 45.7 morning; 45.17 up; 45.21 road; 45.22 harsh; 45.23 time;
45.25 road; 45.26 pleasant; 45.29 wonder; 46.13 involuntarily; 46.15
pale; 46.16 large; 46.19 horns; 46.24 moment; 46.29 Then; 46.30
shoulders; 47.5 before; 47.10 far; 47.12 contrary; 47.13 summer; 47.18
names; 47.18 dark; 47.21 department; 47.22 direction; 47.27 around;
47.28 library; 47.28 that; 47.29 mellow; 47.29 Avenue; 47.30 Hotel;
47.32 racy; 47.32 night; 48.18 her; 48.19 champion; 49.3 statement; 49.6
clever; 49.6 men; 49.10 and; 49.10 unwillingness; 49.11 cool; 49.13 hard;
49.20 careful; 49.30 ahead; 49.31 moment; 49.32 face; 51.3 shore; 51.12
folds; 51.14 names; 51.17 Leeches; 51.18 Bunsen; 51.18 Yale; 51.20
Voltaires; 51.23 wife; 51.24 hair; 51.24 say; 51.29 Schraeders; 52.2 came;
52.2 too; 52.3 Flink; 52.3 Hammerheads; 52.4 importer; 52.7 Orchid;
52.7 Excellence; 52.12 there; 52.13 gamble; 52.25 Palmetto; 52.28
person; 52.31 Consuela; 52.36 Brewer; 52.37 war; 53.2 Hip; 53.3 something; 53.4 Duke; 53.7 o'clock; 53.7 July; 53.10 me; 53.14 today; 53.20
nervous; 53.31 conservatory; 54.5 me; 54.16 Oxford; 54.20 it; 54.20 it;
54.21 doubt; 54.21 pieces; 54.22 him; 54.28 solemn; 54.30 leg; 54.33
only; 55.3 relief; 55.4 die; 55.12 major; 55.17 pocket; 55.20 astonishment;
57.8 blinds; 57.10 Europe; 57.21 outside; 57.24 small; 57.30 me; 57.35
restaurant; 58.2 Wolfshiem; 58.14 table; 58.17 right; 58.17 Rosy; 58.17
up; 58.21 then; 58.26 sidewalk; 58.29 Five; 59.1 arrived; 59.7 Gatsby;
59.11 situation; 59.12 sportswoman; 59.14 up; 59.15 room; 60.10 polite;
60.13 me; 60.20 he; 60.27 knew; 60.27 course; 60.28 1919; 61.10 briefly;
61.20 another; 61.23 wind; 61.24 white; 61.25 *tut-tut-tut-tut*; 61.29
white; 612.29 car; 61.32 anyways; 62.1 Hello; 62.2 me; 62.9 Gatsby;
62.20 more; 62.21 town; 62.26 Chicago; 62.28 cars; 62.32 dinner; 62.35
before; 63.7 maid; 63.9 ball; 63.12 dress; 63.13 later; 63.13 room; 63.15
shiver; 63.17 back; 63.19 uneasily; 63.22 hour; 63.26 night; 63.27 papers;
63.27 too; 63.30 girl; 63.31 Cannes; 63.31 Deauville; 63.37 tongue; 64.7
up; 64.15 Fifties; 64.30 Jordan; 65.4 see; 65.19 Tom's; 65.23 now; 65.25
Suddenly; 65.26 person; 65.27 skepticism; 65.36 trees; 66.1 Buchanan;
66.3 signs; 66.4 wan; 66.4 smiled; 67.4 light; 67.6 corner; 67.11 trees;
68.5 Island; 68.7 morning; 68.13 raincoat; 68.13 lawn-mower; 68.15 tea;
68.20 nervously; 68.20 Gatsby; 68.21 shirt; 68.21 tie; 68.22 pale; 68.26
but; 68.26 expression; 68.32 pantry; 69.1 mist; 69.4 floor; 69.7 me; 69.7
voice; 69.16 up; 69.25 alone; 69.26 cheek; 70.8 wire; 70.12 laugh; 70.15
hall; 70.20 clock; 70.21 Daisy; 70.21 sitting; 70.22 graceful; 70.24 me;
70.27 fingers; 71.8 and; 71.8 talked; 71.9 tense; 71.10 itself; 71.11
moment; 71.15 door; 71.26 that; 71.28 reproach; 71.28 and; 71.28
cautiously; 71.32 tree; 71.33 pouring; 71.36 house; 72.9 hour; 72.9 again;

72.13 each; 72.19 kitchen; 72.21 couch; 72.22 asked; 72.24 tears; 73.28
door; 73.30 inside; 73.31 salons; 74.5 bath; 74.8 Daisy; 74.11 way; 74.16
delight; 74.28 shirts; 74.32 them; 74.32 one; 74.33 flannel; 74.37 green;
74.37 orange; 75.1 Suddenly; 75.1 sound; 75.6 house; 75.6 pool; 75.8
again; 75.13 abruptly; 75.36 rang; 76.15 man; 76.17 sport-shirt; 76.17
sneakers; 76.29 match; 76.30 room; 77.8 change; 77.19 fault; 77.26 hers;
77.28 most; 77.28 warmth; 77.30 me; 78.7 habit; 78.8 Gatsby; 78.17 No;
78.23 Tom; 78.26 polite; 79.5 conversation; 79.30 army; 79.32 porch;
80.5 nod; 80.7 Gatsby; 80.7 hand; 80.12 fact; 80.21 player; 80.23 player;
80.31 Tom; 80.33 orchestras; 80.35 dance; 81.1 floor; 81.2 cider; 81.2
wanted; 81.3 windmill; 81.7 orchestra; 81.8 also; 81.14 enormously;
81.16 evening; 81.22 bright; 81.22 too; 81.37 incredulously; 82.7 group;
82.10 who; 82.11 distance; 82.19 hesitation; 82.21 However; 82.21
Gatsby; 82.27 him; 82.33 incognito; 83.10 Common; 83.11 suddenly;
83.18 week; 84.2 us; 84.14 is; 85.5 table; 85.18 lovely; 85.21 myself;
85.24 way; 85.26 No; 86.20 host; 86.26 off; 87.2 funny; 87.3 in; 87.17
steps; 87.18 all; 87.25 who; 88.3 morning; 88.17 all; 88.20 and; 88.21
begun; 88.22 him; 89.5 others; 89.6 tradesmen; 89.8 pigsty; 91.2 night;
91.2 ago; 91.19 flower; 91.22 somewhere; 91.23 mouth; 91.25 sound;
91.29 Gatsby; 91.31 hottest; 91.36 shirtwaist; 92.19 sorry; 92.19
madame; 93.1 laughed; 93.2 sweet; 93.7 well; 93.9 time; 93.19 down;
93.25 Daisy; 94.14 room; 94.23 Come; 94.28 said; 94.29 long; 95.32
Gatsby; 96.4 town; 97.12 her; 97.23 Jordan; 97.30 snob; 97.34 ale; 97.36
road; 98.5 angrily; 98.20 bad; 98.29 for; 99.9 world; 99.18 disquiet;
99.19 afternoon; 99.21 vigil; 99.25 little; 99.27 observed; 99.32 Tom;
99.34 mind; 100.4 hour; 100.11 Tom; 100.12 stop; 100.15 movies;
100.28 move; 100.32 gate; 100.37 legs; 102.14 it; 102.24 way; 102.33
unpleasant; 103.1 ballroom; 103.17 house; 103.19 pale; 103.28 institutions; 103.30 gibberish; 104.6 you; 104.15 door; 104.20 question; 104.24
limits; 104.33 clergyman; 104.35 said; 105.4 Why; 105.26 myself; 105.32
desire; 106.29 word; 106.33 Why; 106.37 answer; 107.5 triumph; 107.8
Tom; 107.11 care; 107.17 her; 107.29 portentous; 107.33 laughing;
107.35 together; 108.10 garage; 108.12 bed; 108.16 tomorrow; 108.21
working; 108.29 uneasy; 108.29 restaurant; 109.5 moment; 109.12 first;
109.13 shirtwaist; 109.13 perspiration; 109.14 flap; 109.16 corners;
109.22 stopping; 109.32 garage; 109.33 throat; 109.37 again; 110.4
blanket; 110.5 blanket; 110.6 wall; 110.13 attempting; 110.14 time;
110.16 wall; 110.16 again; 110.17 high; 110.18 O; 110.18 O; 110.18 O;
110.18 O; 110.19 and; 110.20 eyes; 111.1 her; 111.13 door; 112.29 said;
112.4 this; 112.6 Now; 112.7 doll; 112.8 chair; 112.20 hard; 112.21 sob;

112.27 floor; 112.33 him; 113.14 day; 113.15 expression; 113.19 house; 113.27 Somehow; 114.3 us; 114.17 until; 114.18 way; 114.19 quick; 114.21 driver; 114.27 stop; 114.32 room; 114.37 night; 115.11 softly; 115.12 porch; 115.13 before; 115.17 table; 115.17 them; 115.18 her; 115.23 picture; 116.4 savage; 116.5 drive; 116.7 about; 116.8 lawn; 116.16 pavilions; 116.19 everywhere; 116.20 musty; 116.21 table; 116.21 stale; 116.23 room; 117.18 part; 117.20 imagination; 117.25 vulgar; 117.30 themselves; 118.3 brown; 118.5 early; 118.9 constant; 118.13 stand; 118.29 robust; 118.34 yacht; 119.15 was; 119.15 turn; 119.15 skipper; 119.17 about; 119.19 years; 119.21 Boston; 119.24 hard; 119.28 things; 119.33 then; 120.1 and; 120.1 gesture; 120.3 thing; 120.10 first; 120.10 days; 120.13 Louisville; 120.13 where; 120.13 night; 120.15 dark; 120.18 people; 120.23 intensity; 120.27 corridors; 120.30 him; 120.30 too; 120.35 past; 121.10 him; 121.16 extraordinary; 121.20 again; 121.20 later; 121.21 was; 121.21 somehow; 121.25 ever; 121.27 clothes; 122.10 room; 122.11 little; 122.12 awhile; 122.14 love; 122.16 shoulder; 122.18 front; 122.20 business; 122.22 home; 122.26 outside; 122.32 pairs; 122.35 low; 123.3 men; 123.11 position; 123.18 slow; 123.19 cool; 123.30 houses; 123.32 harder; 123.35 chair; 124.3 sun; 124.21 work; 125.2 worth; 125.4 steps; 125.5 home; 125.12 city; 125.14 me; 125.19 cool; 125.20 window; 125.22 Hempstead; 125.24 Daisy; 125.25 me; 125.36 awhile; 126.1 click; 126.3 later; 126.6 time-table; 126.11 dust; 126.12 happened; 126.13 longer; 126.18 night; 126.21 this; 126.21 fainted; 126.22 Someone; 126.22 curious; 126.25 garage; 126.27 open; 126.28 shame; 126.29 first; 126.32 that; 127.4 this; 127.5 Oh; 127.13 light; 127.16 garage; 127.17 lying; 128.1 small; 128.1 dog-leash; 128.5 it; 128.9 that; 128.12 Oh; 128.29 too; 128.31 husband; 128.36 again; 129.16 me; 129.17 him; 129.18 Eckleburg; 129.18 emerged; 129.19 enormous; 129.25 out; 129.27 back; 129.28 three; 129.29 now; 129.30 garage; 129.32 Hill; 129.33 eat; 129.34 slowly; 129.36 crazy; 130.4 thereabouts; 130.4 hand; 130.7 Egg; 130.18 little; 130.21 arrived; 130.24 come; 130.36 house; 131.4 gardener; 131.5 I; 131.12 tracing; 132.7 yard; 132.13 eager; 132.19 hers; 132.21 it; 132.30 then; 132.31 speak; 132.31 hour; 133.16 Broadway; 133.17 five; 133.29 questions; 133.33 violence; 133.35 Wolfshiem; 133.37 newspaper; 134.14 Truly; 134.21 man; 134.24 excitement; 134.26 collapse; 134.28 eat; 135.6 room; 135.8 arrived; 135.17 upstairs; 135.29 impressively; 135.30 lived; 135.32 said; 136.3 too; 136.5 crowd; 136.12 course; 136.17 Greenwich; 136.18 fact; 136.20 me; 136.24 see; 136.24 shoes; 136.26 name; 136.30 liquor; 136.34 boy; 136.35 Company; 136.36 vain; 136.37 partition; 137.4 untrue; 137.17

Chicago; 137.24 us; 138.2 appearing; 138.2 man; 138.11 charges; 138.14 friend; 138.18 slightly; 138.25 sentimental; 138.28 funeral; 138.30 gon-negtion; 139.15 home; 140.14 Flushing; 140.18 hall; 140.19 anxiously; 140.19 shocked; 140.20 watch; 140.30 assistants; 141.1 funeral; 141.2 glasses; 141.4 moment; 141.5 away; 141.5 remember; 141.5 anger; 141.16 again; 141.21 evening; 141.22 friends; 141.22 gayeties; 141.27 acquaintances; 142.1 hour; 142.4 towns; 142.4 youth; 142.36 together; 143.1 still; 143.2 listening; 143.3 golf; 143.8 that; 143.9 head; 143.14 now; 143.14 me; 144.3 back; 144.12 word; 144.13 away; 144.16 leave; 144.22 Daisy's; 144.28 sideboard; 144.30 him; 144.34 carelessness; 145.1 necklace; 145.7 accident; 145.12 laughter; 145.12 incessant; 145.12 garden; 145.14 there; 145.22 moonlight; 146.1 old; 146.4 lawn; 146.9 then.

Other accidental variants

The initial reading in each entry below is from the text of *Trimalchio* published in this edition. Unless otherwise indicated, the accidental form of that initial reading–i.e., its punctuation, spelling, capitalization, or word division–is that of the MS. The second (rejected) reading is always that of the base text, which is the printed galley text. Independent editorial emendations are denoted by the siglum "ed". Entries marked with an asterisk are for changes that Fitzgerald himself marked in his set of the galleys.

The following words have been regularized throughout to these forms, which are Fitzgerald's preferred forms (a few of them British). These words do not appear otherwise in the tables:

afterwards, any more, anyone, anything, ash-grey, ash-heap, awhile, center, criticize, dining room, downstairs, drawing room, dressing room, drug store, everybody, everyone, eye-sore, Father (as proper name), finger bowls, forever, glamour, goodbye, good night, grey, halfway, hydroplane, judgements, living room, mad man, motorboat, moving picture, music room, nearby, plum tree, self absorption, self control, self consciously, sitting room, skepticism, somber, someone, swimming pool, taxi cab, time-table, today, tomorrow, upstairs, week-end, well dressed, work table.

5.19	horizon —] ~;		7.18	trees —] ~,
6.33	prep-school] ~^~		7.18	movies —] ~,

7.31	rounded" man.] ~~."	17.6	deaf^] ed; ~,
7.36	York^] ~~	*17.31	fool.'] ~."
8.35	savours] savors	18.25	Oh,–] ~~
9.5	France,] ~^	19.15	heart-to-heart] ~^~^~
9.14	red^and^white] ~~~~	19.24	called^] ~:
9.20	gold,] ~^	20.22	himself–] ~,
9.24	sturdy, straw^haired] ~^	21.6	gardens,] ~;
	~~	21.18	but,] ~^
9.25	shining,] ~^	22.6	off!] ~,
10.2	Senior Society] senior society	22.18	Repairs] *Repairs*
		22.18	Cars Bought and Sold]
10.12	off^shore] offshore		*Cars bought and sold*
10.21	wedding^cake] ~~	22.32	week.] ~;
10.21	ceiling–] ~,	24.4	moving^picture] ~~
11.20	self^sufficiency] ~~	24.4	and,] ~^
11.26	mouth–] ~,	24.5	drug^store,] ~~^
11.37	North Shore] ed; north shore MS, G	24.12	have,] ~~
		24.14	basket,] ~^
12.2	irrelevantly,] ~:	24.14	neck,] ~^
12.20	said^] ~:	24.17	taxi^window] ~~
12.25	complained.] ed; ~,	24.19	dogs.] ~;
12.27	retorted.] ed; ~,	24.24	*police*] police
12.30	pantry.] ed; ~,	24.27	catching] cataching
13.26	helplessly,] ~:	24.30	*That*] That
13.27	answer,] ed; ~^	24.32	airedale] airdale
13.29	exclaimed.] ed; ~;	24.32	airedale] ed; airdale
14.7	here–] ~,	25.6	said.] ed; ~,
14.20	Coloured] Colored	25.14	apartment^houses] ~~
15.1	again, "–and] ~. "–And	25.31	elevator^boy] ~~
15.3	that,] ~~	25.33	dog^biscuits] dog-biscuit
15.26	inside.] ed; ~,	26.1	afternoon,] ~;
15.27	her^] ~.	26.10	–after] (~
15.30	confirmation.] ~:	26.11	names–] ~)
16.2	orward,] ~^	26.12	apartment^door] ~~
*16.9	know?] ~,	26.34	cream^colored] ~~
16.23	continued,] ~:	26.37	vitality,] ~^
16.26	her voice sang^] Her ~~:	27.1	garage,] ~^
16.26	"–It's romantic. Isn't] "It's ~, isn't	27.13	McKee.] ed; ~,
		27.18	*on*] on
16.29	startlingly] startlingly	27.30	Sh!] *Sh,*

28.9	the Gulls] The ~
28.10	the Sea] The ~
29.10	see?] ~,
29.15	*do*] do
29.24	Marseilles] ed; Marseille
29.33	me^] ~:
29.34	*way*] way
29.36	down.] ed; ~,
29.36	At] at
30.10	him?] ~!
30.12	there!] ~.
31.7	shirt^front] ~–~
31.7	arm–] ~,
31.11	forever,] ~;
31.17	ash^trays] ~–~
*31.18	spring,] ~^
32.8	Versailles] ed; Versaille
32.16	dignity.] ed; ~,
33.9	city,] ~^
33.13	garden^shears] ~–~
33.19	hour,] ~^
33.24	hors^d'oeuvre] ~–~
33.30	arrived–] ~,
33.30	five^piece] ~–~
33.31	saxophones] ed; saxaphones
34.5	Castile] ed; Castille
34.12	easier,] ~^
34.15	breath–] ~;
34.35	party,] ~^
34.37	robin's^egg] ~–~
35.2	employer–] ~:
35.8	ill-at-ease] ~^~^~
35.19	garden] oarden
36.30	alert,] ~^
37.22	sometime] sometimes
37.22	*bet*] bet
38.27	host–] ~:
39.15	See?] ~!
39.34	den,] ~;
40.10	"twins"–] ^~^,
41.30	girl's^] ~:
41.36	Vladimir] Vladimr
42.2	added^] ~:
42.3	whereupon] Whereupon
42.11	low^brow] ~–~
42.15	weird,] ~^
43.12	*me?*] me?
43.16	evening^dress] ~–~
43.25	red^haired] ~–~
43.33	heavily^beaded] ~–~
44.10	hissed^] ~:
44.36	phone] 'phone
45.28	him–] ~,
46.3	indignantly.] ed; ~,
46.5	bystanders] by-standers
46.25	sky.^] ed; ~."
46.31	Wonder'ff] Wonder^'ff
46.36	*off*] off
47.31	Station] ed; station
49.10	disadvantage,] ~^
49.32	slow^thinking] ~–~
51.7	von] ed; Von
53.1	Peters,] ~^
53.14	said. "You're] ed; ~, "you're
53.17	daytime;] ~–
53.27	wind-shields] ~^~
53.26	decided.] ed; ~;
55.4	to] toñ
55.20	*Orderi di Danilo …]* Orderi di Danilo … The entire inscription is in italics in MS.
56.24	faded^gilt] ~–~
57.4	olfactory] ed; oleofactory
57.10	south-eastern] southeastern
57.12	Blackwells] Blackwell's
57.14	yolks] ed; yokes

57.21	ante-room] anteroom	66.4	again,] ~^
57.26	half^darkness] ~-~	67.15	world's fair] World's Fair
57.27	him–] ~,	68.16	white-washed]
57.28	–and] and		whitewashed
57.32	sid,] ~:	68.21	gold^colored] ~-~
58.1	headwaiter] head^waiter	69.1	half^past] ~-~
58.24	went,] ~^	69.18	lilac^trees] ~-~
58.25	indignantly–] ~.	69.28	me?] ~,
58.25	says,] ~:	69.28	ear.] ed; ~,
58.32	me.] ~:	69.28	Or] or
58.37	Wolfshiem.] ed; ~,	69.32	murmur,] ~:
59.7	me.] ~,	70.1	funny!] ~,
*59.21	Oh.] Oh, MS; Oh! G	70.3	light,] ~^
60.13	hand——] ~.	70.13	note.] ~:
60.20	anyhow–] ~,	71.16	whispered^] ~:
60.31	singlemindedness] single-	71.30	way,] ~—
	mindedness	71.31	before,] ~—
61.3	said.] ed; ~;	72.16	little, ... then,] ~^ ... ~^
61.15	Gatsby——] ~.	73.1	said.] ed; ~,
61.31	night, "anyways] ~.	73.31	salons] ed; Salons
	"Anyways	74.3	Klipspringer]
62.34	sauterne] Sauterne		Klippspringer
62.35	'Gratulate] ^~	74.18	when] When
62.36	oh,] ~^	74.27	dressing^gowns] ~-~
63.1	you.] ~;	74.34	many-colored] ~-^~
63.2	dearis^] deares'	74.37	apple^green] ~-~
63.5	Say^] ~:	75.6	grounds] gounds
63.10	soap^dish] ~-~	75.31	it!] ed; ~,
63.19	say^] ~:	76.12	Gatsby.] ed; ~,
63.36	hard^drinking] ~-~	76.12	We'll] we'll
64.13	Victoria] victoria	76.17	sport-shirt] ~^~
64.18	*I'm the Sheik* ...] I'm the	77.1	Gatsby.] ed; ~,
	Sheik	77.1	Play] play
	The entire song lyric is	77.2	*"In the morning* ...] "In
	in italics in MS.		the morning
64.30	know–] ~,		Both sections of the
64.30	–if] ed; ^~		lyric that appear in this
65.3	afraid. He's] ed; ~, he's		chapter are in italics in
65.16	mad.] ~:		MS.
65.29	pursuing,] ~;	77.11	*children,*] ~.

78.7	riding^habit] ~-~
79.10	Certainly.] ~;
80.19	Good^looking] ~-~
80.24	Yes,] ~;
81.1	knee^deep] ~-~
81.2	field^hand] ~-~
81.3	straw^covered] ~-~
81.3	outside,] ~^
81.15	cooperated] co-operated
81.20	dinner^coat] ~-~
82.4	said. And] ed; ~, and
82.19	after] ed; After
82.19	added,] ~:
82.36	danced;] ~—
83.2	rite–] ~;
83.6	elsewhere–] ~,
83.10	she.] ~?
83.24	bounded, ... satisfaction,] ~^ ... ~^
83.34	ear^drum] ~-~
84.36	him,] ~^
85.16	And,] ~^
86.24	Well–"] ed; ~"–
86.34	him; then] ~. Then
87.11	yes. Some] ~, some
87.13	night,] ~—
87.23	at,] ~^
91.35	combustion] ed; combusion
92.21	was^] ~:
92.28	idols,] ~^
98.8	And] and
93.11	No,] ~^
93.18	Gatsby,] ~^
93.34	say^] ~—
94.34	Gatsby.] ed; ~,
95.5	rosebeds] ~-~
95.6	dog^days] dogdays
95.11	darkened, too,] ~^ ~^
95.20	moulding] molding

96.7	onto] on^to
96.20	Oh.] ~!
96.27	trembling.] ~:
97.30	Tom, if] Tom. If
97.32	him. She] ~; she
97.34	and, ... it,] ~^ ... ~^
98.32	does!] ~,
100.16	complained.] ~."
101.12	said.] ed; ~,
101.12	We'll] we'll
101.15	casually,] ~:
102.25	Tom.] ed; ~,
102.25	Sometime] sometime
102.33	mirror.] ed; ~,
102.33	If] if
103.33	Jordan.] ed; ~,
103.33	Except] except
104.36	on?^] ~?–
106.37	Tom.] ed; ~:
109.2	shouting;] ~—
109.4	car,] ~^
109.11	thick,] ~^
109.22	down,] ~^
109.29	of^] ~:
109.34	violent,] ~^
110.18	O ... O ... O ... O] Oh ... Oh ... Oh ... Oh
110.33	Michaelis.] ed; ~,
110.33	One] one
110.36	she–"] ~"–
110.37	side, "–she] ~—"~
111.6	said.] ed; ~,
111.6	Big] big
111.6	^New] "~
111.14	cries.] ~:
111.25	little,] ~.
111.28	hear?] ~.
112.9	him!] ~,
112.36	home. And] ~, and
113.3	¶He] ^~

113.4	¶"Come] ^"~	133.26	brain.] ~:
113.12	half^past] ~-~	134.7	*Dear Mr. Carraway*]
113.36	so.] ~;		Dear Mr. Carraway
114.21	thing,] ~—		The entire letter is in
115.5	house:] ~;		italics in MS.
115.8	said.] ed; ~,	134.14	*Truly*^] truly,
115.37	moonlight,] ~—	134.15	*WOLFSHIEM*^] ~.
118.2	clam^digger] ~-~	134.17	*etc.*^] etc.;
118.2	salmon^fisher] ~-~	135.1	coffee,] ~?
118.18	college] College	135.2	sandwich?] ed; ~.
118.27	seventy] Seventy	135.3	Mr.] ~^
118.29	softmindedness] soft- mindedness	135.36	frightened–] ~:
		136.2	Oh–] ~!
119.25	sea-board] seaboard	136.21	nervously.] ~:
119.37	moment.] ed; ~,	137.16	sickintired] sick in tired
122.7	going] ed; doing	137.18	Gatsby.] ~!
122.20	machine^guns] ~-~	137.19	Oh-h–] Oh-h!
122.32	"Beale Street Blues" [ed; ^Beale Street blues^ MS, G	138.2	fine^appearing] ~-~
		138.6	everything–"] ~"–
		138.7	fingers"–] ~—"
122.32	pairs] pair	139.22	here. This] ~, this
124.19	train.] ~,	139.25	fly-leaf] flyleaf
125.13	swivel^chair] ~-~	139.26	12th] 12
125.19	golf^links] ~-~	140.3	parents.] ~^
125.28	Then–] ~:	140.15	look] ed; lo9k
126.29	him–] ~;	140.25	and, ... later,] ~^ ... ~^
127.32	half^cunning] ~-~	141.21	Station] station
127.32	half^bewildered] ~-~	141.24	This^or^That's] ~-~-~
128.25	definitely.] ed; ~,	142.34	in] ed; n
129.13	window–"] ~"–	143.17	remember–"] ~"–
129.14	it, "–and] ~-^"~	143.17	"–a] –"~
129.29	sleep. When] ~; when	144.24	unutterable] unatterable
130.4	thereabouts] thereabout	145.8	about] abou^t
130.5	forward–] ~,	146.1	there,] ~^
130.9	bathing^suit] ~-~	146.11	morning——] ~!——

Factual readings

The readings below are factual inconsistencies in the text of *Trimalchio*. None of these readings has been altered for this edition; only errors that were revised by Fitzgerald in galleys have been emended. *Trimalchio*, as a work of fiction, need not be absolutely congruent with reality. Attention to factual matters is given in the Cambridge edition of *The Great Gatsby* (intro., pp. xliv-xlvi; substantive emendations, pp. 143–54; and appendix 4, "Note on Geography"). The issue is addressed as well in the Cambridge editions of *This Side of Paradise* and *Flappers and Philosophers*, pp. xliv-xlvi and xxvi–xxvii.

12.4   **three years old** Daisy's and Tom's daughter should probably be two: they were married in the spring of 1919, and the child was born in April 1920. This scene is set in June 1922. See the readings at 62.25 and 63.30.

21.18   **retinas** Fitzgerald might have meant *irises*, since the retina is at the back of the eyeball and cannot normally be seen. He might in fact have wanted *retinas*, however, for its sound. Fitzgerald apparently knew the meaning of *irises*; he used the word correctly in the first sentence of his 1920 story "The Offshore Pirate," collected in *Flappers and Philosophers*: "This unlikely story begins on a sea that was a blue dream, as colorful as blue silk stockings, and beneath a sky as blue as the irises of children's eyes" (Cambridge edition, p. 5).

23.21   **the lower level** In a 24 March 1925 letter, Fitzgerald's friend Ring Lardner suggested a change here: "There ain't any lower level in that station," he noted. Trains from Long Island, however, did arrive in an area designated "Long Island Station," a space below 33rd Street in Pennsylvania Station. This is likely the "lower level" that Fitzgerald had in mind; he also mentions the "cold lower level" of Penn Station at 32.24.

30.28   **eastward** To reach Central Park from Myrtle's apartment on West 158th Street, Nick would have had to walk both south, at least to 110th Street, and east.

62.29   **Mulbach Hotel** Fitzgerald was perhaps confusing the Muehlebach Hotel in Kansas City with the Seelbach Hotel in Louisville.

141.20 **La Salle Street Station** The Chicago, Milwaukee & St. Paul Railroad ran from Union Station in Chicago.

Hyphenated compounds

The compound words in the table below are hyphenated at the ends of lines in the Cambridge text. The hyphens should be preserved when quoting these words. All other compound words hyphenated at the ends of lines should be quoted as a single word.

10.21 wine-colored; 13.1 sun-strained; 16.16 dinner-time; 35.21 passers-by; 39.6 as-ascertain [Owl-eyes is stumbling over the word.]; 65.36 Fifty-ninth; 68.16 white-washed; 74.34 many-colored; 86.12 table-cloth; 98.7 hollow-eyed; 119.25 sea-board; 123.27 out-of-the-way.

EXPLANATORY NOTES

Annotated here are references in *Trimalchio* to persons, places, social customs, works of popular music, and events unfamiliar to contemporary (and especially international) readers of Fitzgerald's works.

6.24   graduated from New Haven

Nick means Yale University in New Haven, Connecticut. Fitzgerald had attended Princeton University, but in his fiction he often had his protagonists matriculate at Yale.

9.2   Lake Forest

A suburb of Chicago located along the northern shore of Lake Michigan. The area is characterized by wooded bluffs, deep ravines, and winding roads; homes of the wealthy are located throughout Lake Forest. Fitzgerald's first serious love, Ginevra King, lived there.

10.2   Senior Society

Each of the six senior societies at Yale elected fifteen men to membership at the end of their third years. To be elected to one of the societies, and especially to the prestigious Skull and Bones, was an important honor.

11.37   North Shore

The northern shore of Lake Michigan, where suburbs for the wealthy were located. See the annotation for Lake Forest above.

14.19   'The Rise of the Coloured Empires'

Tom misremembers the title and author (though Fitzgerald might have changed both deliberately because he was referring to a book published by

Charles Scribner's Sons). Tom has been reading *The Rising Tide of Color against White World-Supremacy* by Lothrop Stoddard, published by Scribners in 1920, with an introduction by Madison Grant. Stoddard, a Harvard Ph.D., predicts a racial world war if the migration of Asians and Africans to western nations is not stemmed by a revision of the Versailles treaty. The anthropologist Franz Boas called the book "vicious propaganda" (*Nation*, Dec. 1920); other reviewers judged the argument "highly dangerous" and "the work of a pseudo-scientist with a considerable skill in writing." Tom's comment—"It's all scientific stuff; it's been proved."—refers to the appearance of the volume, which is fitted out with maps and footnotes. Fitzgerald probably knew of the book because it was published by Scribners in the same month (April) that the firm published his first novel, *This Side of Paradise*.

16.25   Cunard or White Star Line

Two British transatlantic passenger lines. The best-known Cunard liners were the *Mauretania*, the *Aquitania*, and the *Berengaria*; the most famous White Star liners (known for their distinctive black-topped funnels) were the *Olympic*, the *Brittanic*, and the ill-fated *Titanic*. The two lines merged in the 1930s.

18.10   "Saturday Evening Post"

The most popular magazine in the country at the time, specializing in short fiction. Fitzgerald published over sixty short stories in the *Post* during his career.

18.24   Westchester

Jordan will play on a golf course in Westchester County, an area north of New York City containing suburbs for the well-to-do.

18.27   rotogravure

An early intaglio process for printing photographs in newspapers and magazines. The "rotogravure" section of a newspaper was an illustrated supplement, often featuring images of movie stars, stage personalities, and sports figures. Because of Jordan's fame as a golfer, Nick would have seen her photograph there.

18.28   Asheville ... Hot Springs ... Palm Beach

Resorts for the wealthy in North Carolina, Arkansas, and Florida. All three were known for their golf courses; this is why Nick thinks of Jordan's name in conjunction with them.

25.28   "Town Tattle"

Fitzgerald probably had in mind the journal *Town Topics*, owned (until his death in 1920) by Colonel William D'Alton Mann, who founded the *Smart Set*, edited by Fitzgerald's friends H. L. Mencken and George Jean Nathan. *Town Topics* was primarily a gossip magazine; its most popular section, called "Saunterings," consisted of scandalous material about the celebrated and wealthy. The journal also published witty reviews and light short stories.

25.29   "Simon Called Peter"

A popular, scandalous British novel by Robert Keable (1887–1927), published successfully in the United States by E. P. Dutton in 1921. The protagonist, an army chaplain, goes to the front where he loses his ideals and morals. His adventures are described more graphically than was customary in the 1920s. ("Almost the next second Julie appeared in the doorway. She was still half-wet from the water, and her sole dress was a rosebud which she had just tucked into her hair" [Dutton edn., p. 287].) In letters to Perkins, Fitzgerald worried about including this mention of Keable's novel in his text but eventually decided to retain the passage.

28.9   Montauk Point

The easternmost tip of Long Island, known for the beauty of its natural scenery and for its lighthouse.

32.25   Pennsylvania Station

Penn Station was the largest train terminal in Manhattan. It occupied the two city blocks bounded by 33rd Street, Seventh Avenue, 31st Street, and Eighth Avenue. Its architect, Charles Follen McKim, modelled the structure on the Baths of Caracalla. Penn Station was demolished in 1965.

32.25 "Tribune"

This New York newspaper took a conservative political stance in the 1920s; traditional ideas might be what Nick wishes to read after the party at Myrtle's apartment. Later the *Tribune* was acquired by Frank Munsey's New York *Herald* to form the *Herald-Tribune*.

34.22 moving her hands like Frisco

Joe Frisco (1889–1958), a comedian and dancer, was just beginning to enjoy wide popularity in the early 1920s. He was known for his stuttering delivery of laugh lines and for his eccentric movements when performing the "Frisco Dance," a soft-shoe shuffle done to the music of "Dark Town Strutter's Ball." In the 1920s he was featured in the Ziegfeld productions at a popular night spot called the Midnight Frolic (see the note that follows immediately). He was also a headliner in Earl Carroll's *Vanities*, a variety show. Later in his career he performed a Jewish version of the Charleston.

34.25 Gilda Gray's understudy from the Follies

Gilda Gray, a dancer and cabaret singer, has been credited with inventing the Shimmy. ("I'm shaking my shimmy, that's what I'm doing.") The *Follies*, a Broadway review featuring pretty girls and elaborate sets and costumery, was produced each year by the impresario Florenz Ziegfeld. Gilda Gray starred in the *Follies* during the early 1920s; she also performed regularly at the Midnight Frolic, a roof garden atop the New Amsterdam Theater at 214 West 42nd Street.

38.6 Eton and Groton ... Andovah

The character, whose "Oxford mush-mouth" accent Fitzgerald is satirizing, has entered his son in advance for admission to two prestigious schools, one in England and the other in the United States. Eton College (est. 1440) is in Eton, Buckinghamshire, on the Thames; Groton School (est. 1884) is in Groton, Massachusetts. The traditions and rules at Groton during this period were based on English models. "Andovah" is Phillips Academy in Andover, Massachusetts (est. 1780), the oldest boys' preparatory school in New England. The atmosphere at Andover was consciously democratic; hence the character's remark about snobbishness.

38.15   the glass parlors at Westover

Westover (est. 1909) was a small, prestigious country boarding school for girls near Middlebury, Connecticut. Boys who paid visits to the girls there were allowed to sit with them only in glassed-in parlors, where activities could be monitored by chaperones. Fitzgerald was familiar with the glass parlors at Westover; his first serious love, Ginevra King, attended the school, and he visited her there in February 1915.

38.22   "limbs" ... legs

During the late Victorian period it was thought improper in some circles to use the word "legs" in polite conversation; one referred to "limbs" instead. Jordan's friends consider the movie star's use of "limbs" to be quaint.

39.14   "Stoddard Lectures"

John L. Stoddard (1850–1931) was a popular public lecturer, one of the first to use a stereopticon in his presentations. He traveled widely and published his lectures in a uniformly bound, ten-volume, illustrated series called *John L. Stoddard's Lectures*—first issued in 1897, with five supplementary volumes in 1901. Such a multi-volume series, aimed at a middlebrow audience, is what one would expect a book supplier to have provided, en bloc, for Gatsby's library.

39.16   Belasco

David Belasco (1853–1931) was a famous Broadway dramatist, producer, and director whose greatest successes came before World War I. He was known for the realistic illusions created by his sets—hence the reference here by Owl-eyes. Belasco's best-known productions were *Lord Chumley* and *The Girl of the Golden West*.

41.37   Carnegie Hall

A well-known auditorium in New York City at Seventh Avenue and 57th Street. Carnegie Hall was used mostly for performances of classical music, but some early works of serious jazz—George Gershwin's "Rhapsody in Blue" (1923), for example—were performed there. Having the "Jazz

History of the World" debut at Carnegie Hall would suggest that it is serious music, not cabaret jazz.

43.6   the lower east side

Nick is suggesting that Gatsby might come from humble origins. The Lower East Side of Manhattan was a tenement region, inhabited chiefly by immigrant workers and their families; from time to time someone from the area would rise to prominence, often as a businessman or an entertainer.

43.6   Galena, Illinois

The reference is to Ulysses S. Grant (1822–85), the last commander-in-chief of the Union forces in the Civil War and the eighteenth President of the United States (1869–77). Grant was forced to resign from the army in 1854 for excessive drinking. He failed at farming and business and, at the beginning of the Civil War, was working in obscurity as a clerk in a family leather store in Galena, Illinois. He was commissioned as colonel of the 21st Illinois Volunteers and rose rapidly to the command of all federal forces in the West. In March 1864, Abraham Lincoln appointed him commander-in-chief. Fitzgerald would use the allusion again in *Tender Is the Night*; in the last paragraph of the novel, Nicole hopes that Dick's career "was biding its time" like "Grant's in Galena."

45.24   duster

A long, lightweight overcoat worn by drivers and their passengers in early automobiles for protection against dirt and engine exhaust.

47.24   Yale Club

The Yale Club, at 50 Vanderbilt Avenue (the corner of Vanderbilt and East 44th Street), is a private club used mostly by graduates of the university. It is located near Grand Central Station and, in the twenties, was close to Delmonico's, a fashionable restaurant.

47.30   old Murray Hill Hotel

A traditional hotel, late Victorian in architecture and decor, with one entrance on Park Avenue opposite the raised motor roadway around

Grand Central Station and the other entrance on 40th Street. A contemporary guidebook to New York describes the atmosphere as "heavily gracious"; Nick's mention of the Murray Hill here suggests old, elite, late nineteenth-century New York society. (The Plaza Hotel, where Tom and Gatsby will later have their confrontation, was a much newer and more fashionable hotel than the Murray Hill.) Nick, walking south on Madison Avenue, would not have passed directly in front of the Murray Hill but would have seen it from a short distance, on his left, as he crossed 40th Street.

48.37   she had moved her ball

To understand the import of the accusation one should know that amateur golf in the United States in the 1920s was considered a sport of the upper classes—rather as tennis and polo were—and that the amateur status of golf was zealously guarded. Professional golfers (defined as those who either played for prize money or gave lessons to amateurs) were not even allowed to enter the members' areas of the clubhouses on most golf courses. To cheat in a big tournament by moving one's ball to improve a bad lie would be approximately comparable, in upper-crust circles, to Wolfshiem's alleged fixing of the World's Series, since baseball was thought of as a middle- and lower-class sport.

51.7   von Hindenburg

Paul von Hindenburg (1847–1934) was field marshal of the German forces during World War I; later he was president of Germany from 1925 to 1934.

55.2   Bois de Boulogne

A wooded area of over 2,000 acres lying just west of Paris, adjacent to the wealthy residential districts of Neuilly, Auteuil, and Passy. "Le Bois" was created in the 1850s by Napoleon III as a playground for the upper classes; by the early 1900s it had become a public park frequented by the bourgeoisie. Amusements included rowing, riding, and picnicking.

55.5   Argonne Forest

This was the final and arguably the most important of the campaigns fought by the American Expeditionary Force in World War I. The fighting occurred from late September to mid-November of 1918 in southeastern France, twenty miles north of Verdun. The American effort was massive: it involved 1.2 million men, supported by artillery and supplies. The success of the U.S. troops, on the offensive against well-fortified German defenders, had much to do with bringing about the Armistice that ended the war on 11 November.

55.9   Lewis guns

One-man air-cooled machine guns with circular cartridge drums, used by American soldiers during World War I.

55.25   Trinity Quad

A quadrangle in Trinity College, Oxford University.

55.31   his palace on the Grand Canal

The main thoroughfare of Venice, winding like an inverted letter S through the city, and known to Venetians as the Canalazzo. The Grand Canal is lined by opulent palaces, erected by the city's most wealthy families.

57.12   Blackwells Island

This island, in the East River, was the site of a prison and a charity hospital. Its name was formally changed to Welfare Island in 1921, but it continued to be known as Blackwells Island.

58.10   Metropole

A Manhattan hotel near Broadway and 43rd where the gangster Herman Rosenthal was shot to death in 1912—the murder on which Fitzgerald bases Wolfshiem's recollections in the following paragraphs.

60.24   the man who fixed the World's Series

Fitzgerald based Meyer Wolfsheim on a racketeer and gambler named Arnold Rothstein (1882–1928), who was alleged to have fixed the World's Series in 1919—the famous "Black Sox" scandal of that year. Two players from the Chicago White Sox team (the American League champions) tried to arrange the fix; Rothstein was approached for front money, but he declined to participate. Thus made aware of the probable fix, Rothstein put his money on Cincinnati, the National League pennant winners, and was said to have won over $300,000. The White Sox did lose the Series, and the scandal was exposed. Rothstein was not formally charged with involvement; nevertheless, he became known as the man who fixed the World's Series in 1919. Rothstein was murdered in 1928; the killer was never identified. For details see Leo Katcher, *The Big Bankroll: The Life and Times of Arnold Rothstein* (New York: Harper and Brothers, 1959).

61.19   Plaza Hotel

The Plaza, then as now, was among the most fashionable of the New York caravansaries. It stands at Fifth Avenue and 59th Street, across from the southeast corner of Central Park. The first Plaza Hotel opened in October 1890; it was demolished fifteen years later and the present structure, French Renaissance in style, was opened in 1907.

63.31   Cannes ... Deauville

Cannes, on the French Riviera, was a fashionable wintering-place for British aristocrats during the nineteenth century; by the 1920s it had begun to attract well-known writers, artists, and stage performers as well. Deauville, a seaside resort in Normandy, was a chic watering-hole for the French bourgeoisie; it was known for its boardwalk, casino, and race-course.

64.13   Victoria

Nick and Jordan are riding through Central Park in a rented, horse-drawn carriage. A Victoria was a low, light vehicle with a calash top; there was a perch for the driver in front and a padded seat for passengers in the rear.

64.18   *Sheik of Araby*

From a popular song of 1921, "The Sheik of Araby," with music by Ted Snyder and lyrics by Harry B. Smith and Francis Wheeler. Romantic young men during the twenties were known as "sheiks." The reference also calls to mind *The Sheik*, a popular 1921 movie starring Rudolph Valentino (1895–1926), the first of the "Latin lover" screen idols.

67.17   Coney Island

This large, brightly lit amusement park, built along the seashore at the foot of Brooklyn, was sometimes called a "pyrotechnic insanitarium." It provided release from the rigors of urban life, principally for the working classes. Coney Island could be dangerous: it was frequented also by gamblers, con artists, and petty criminals.

69.3   Clay's "Economics"

Henry Clay (1883–1954) was a British economist and lecturer; his *Economics: An Introduction for the General Reader*, first published in the U.S. in 1918, was praised for its practicality and lucidity. The book was influential in broadening public interest in economic matters. It might be significant that Gatsby looks through the book with "vacant eyes," since Clay was concerned chiefly with the redistribution of wealth for the public good.

69.30   Castle Rackrent

The English novel of this title, by Maria Edgeworth (1767–1849), was first published in 1800. It recounts the high-spirited adventures of three generations of Rackrents, Irish landowners who squander their funds and eventually lose their tumbledown castle. *Castle Rackrent* has been called the first regional historical novel written in English.

71.37   Kant at his church steeple

The German philosopher Immanuel Kant (1724–1804) was said to gaze at a church steeple visible from his writing room as he contemplated metaphysical matters. Kant's insistence that knowledge is limited to the world of phenomena, and that all attempts by man to know things-in-themselves (or noumena) will fail, is a theme of the novel and perhaps significant in this passage.

73.34   "the Merton College Library"

Merton, dating from 1264, was one of the first Oxford colleges to be founded; its Upper Library is among the oldest and most beautiful library buildings in England.

76.17 "sport-shirt" ... duck trousers

Klipspringer is in casual attire. A sport shirt (the term was new then) was a collared garment worn without a tie; duck trousers were made of plain-weave heavy cotton fabric, usually off-white or khaki in color.

76.30 there was no light ... from the hall

An allusion to Keats's "Ode to a Nightingale," lines 38–9: "But here there is no light, / Save what from heaven is with the breezes blown." Fitzgerald took the title for *Tender Is the Night* from Keats's poem and used this passage as the epigraph for the novel.

76.33 "The Love Nest"

A popular 1920 song, with music by Lewis A. Hirsch and lyrics by Otto Harbach.

77.2 *"In the morning ..."*

Lyrics from "Ain't We Got Fun?"—a popular tune of 1921 with words by Gus Kahn and Raymond B. Egan and music by Richard A. Whiting.

88.15 underground pipe-line

During Prohibition it was said that an underground pipeline was being used to run liquor across the Canadian border into the United States. Much illegal alcohol was in fact trucked across from Canada, since the sale and consumption of liquor was legal in that country.

91.27 half holiday

Public half holidays, common in the 1920s, freed workers from their jobs after a morning's labor.

91.33 National Biscuit Company

Nick hears the whistle from the Nabisco bakery, then located in the borough of Queens.

94.14   gin rickeys

An iced drink, usually served during the hot months, containing gin, lime juice, sugar, and soda water.

96.24   "Shall we take anything to drink?"

Prohibition was instituted in January 1919 by the 18th Amendment to the U.S. Constitution. If the members of the party want to drink (conveniently) in New York, they must take their liquor with them and find a private place to consume it—unless they wish to visit a speakeasy. The need for a place to drink helps to explain their decision to take a room at the Plaza, though no one opens the bottle during the scene there.

98.5   Tom threw on both brakes

Most automobiles of the period were equipped with pedal-operated brakes, which acted on the transmission shaft, and hand brakes acting on the hubs of the rear wheels. Later in the novel, Gatsby stops his car (which Daisy is driving) by pulling on the hand brakes.

98.24   straining at the handle

Gasoline pumps during this period were operated by turning a large crank, as Wilson is doing here.

100.4   the elevated

The elevated electric railway lines in New York City (on Second, Third, Sixth, and Ninth Avenues) were often criticized as unsightly; the tracks ran atop frameworks of steel girders.

100.31   park gate ... low wall

Nick and Jordan have purchased popcorn from a vendor at the entrance to Central Park at Fifth Avenue and 59th Street, across from the Plaza Hotel. The park was surrounded by a low wall on which visitors often sat.

102.10 "Wedding March"

This march, from Mendelssohn's incidental music for *A Midsummer Night's Dream*, is frequently used as a processional at weddings.

106.19 Kapiolani . . . the Punch Bowl

Kapiolani is a park on Oahu, one of the Hawaiian islands; the Punch Bowl is a mountain on that same island.

117.31 Tin-Pan Alley

A genre of American music popular in the late nineteenth and early twentieth centuries. The music took its name from a byname for 28th Street between Fifth Avenue and Broadway, where many sheet-music publishing businesses were located. As one walked down the street, one could reportedly hear the tinny sound of pianos being pounded by the "song pluggers" as they demonstrated tunes to the publishers. Irving Berlin and George M. Cohan had their first musical successes on Tin-Pan Alley.

118.18 St. Olaf's

The small, conservative St. Olaf College in Northfield, Minnesota, was founded in 1874 by Norwegian Lutheran immigrants. Nick puts the college in the northern part of Minnesota, but it is located in the southern part of the state.

118.33 Madame de Maintenon

Madame de Maintenon (1635–1719), a woman of modest origins, eventually became the second wife of Louis XIV of France. Pious and narrow-minded, she had much influence over the king during the last years of his reign; some historians have called her scheming and manipulative.

119.13 Barbary Coast

Fitzgerald probably meant the Barbary Coast region of San Francisco, an area of bars, strip joints, and gambling parlors.

122.21   "Beale Street Blues"

A popular and famous early blues tune first published by the pianist and songwriter W. C. Handy (1873–1958) in 1917.

125.22   Hempstead ... Southampton

Hempstead was a community for the well-to-do in east central Long Island. Southampton was a vacation spot on the south shore of Long Island east of Shinnecock Bay, an area then known for its scenery and isolation.

126.4   an exasperated central

Telephones in the early 1920s were not equipped with dialing mechanisms. Instead one gave the number to a central operator, who placed the call through a switchboard. Long distance calls were expensive and required preparation; the line had to be cleared in advance through several intermediate exchanges.

135.30   James J. Hill

This railroad executive and financier (1838–1916) was a self-made man and a hero to many midwestern boys of the time. His base of operations was St. Paul, Minnesota, Fitzgerald's home city; his mansion there, at 240 Summit Avenue, contained thirty-two rooms, a ballroom, and a two-story art gallery.

136.16   Greenwich

A residential town in southwestern Connecticut on Long Island Sound; many well-to-do business executives lived there.

139.21   "Hopalong Cassidy"

Clarence E. Mulford created this upright cowboy hero in 1907; Mulford's *Hopalong Cassidy* was first published in Chicago by McClurg in 1910. Fitzgerald would have known the book as a teenager. The date of 1906 written in Gatsby's copy of the book is an anachronism.

ILLUSTRATIONS

Diamond Dick

and the First Law of Woman

By F. Scott Fitzgerald

Illustrations by James Montgomery Flagg

1. The initial page of the tearsheets of "Diamond Dick and the First Law of Woman," a 1924 story from which Fitzgerald took two paragraphs of description for reuse in the novel. He boxed the paragraphs and marked them "Used in Gatsby" in the right margin. The lines, rewritten, appear in this edition of *Trimalchio* (pp. 122–23), in the first edition of *The Great Gatsby* (p. 134), and in the Cambridge *Gatsby* (pp. 86–7). Princeton University Libraries.

2. Detail from Chapter 1, leaf 12, of the holograph. The typist's eye might have skipped from "moments" at the end of line 3 to "listening" at the beginning of line 5, thus omitting the line "on the threshold, dazzled by the alabaster light," from the transcription. See Appendix 3 of this edition. Princeton University Libraries.

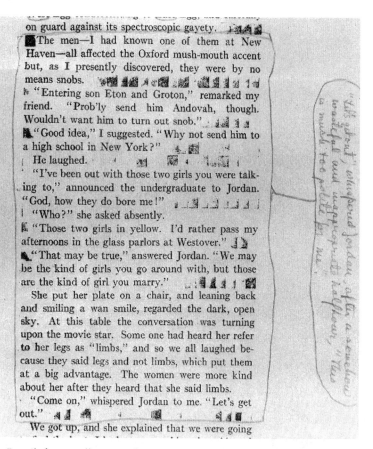

on guard against its spectroscopic gayety.

The men—I had known one of them at New Haven—all affected the Oxford mush-mouth accent but, as I presently discovered, they were by no means snobs.

"Entering son Eton and Groton," remarked my friend. "Prob'ly send him Andovah, though. Wouldn't want him to turn out snob."

"Good idea," I suggested. "Why not send him to a high school in New York?"

He laughed.

"I've been out with those two girls you were talking to," announced the undergraduate to Jordan. "God, how they do bore me!"

"Who?" she asked absently.

"Those two girls in yellow. I'd rather pass my afternoons in the glass parlors at Westover."

"That may be true," answered Jordan. "We may be the kind of girls you go around with, but those are the kind of girl you marry."

She put her plate on a chair, and leaning back and smiling a wan smile, regarded the dark, open sky. At this table the conversation was turning upon the movie star. Some one had heard her refer to her legs as "limbs," and so we all laughed because they said legs and not limbs, which put them at a big advantage. The women were more kind about her after they heard that she said limbs.

"Come on," whispered Jordan to me. "Let's get out."

We got up, and she explained that we were going

3. Detail from galley 14, showing Fitzgerald's revisions. The passage, about Americans who use quasi-British accents, was not included in *The Great Gatsby*; it appears on p. 38 of this edition of *Trimalchio*. Princeton University Libraries.

4. Tommy Hitchcock, on whom the character of Tom Buchanan is partly based. Hitchcock, a flyer in the Lafayette Escadrille, became an investment banker after the war. He was the best polo player of his generation in the U.S. Fitzgerald knew Hitchcock on Long Island during the period that he and Zelda lived in Great Neck, October 1922–April 1924. Fitzgerald also modeled the character Tommy Barban in *Tender Is the Night* in part on Hitchcock. Photo courtesy Museum of Polo and Hall of Fame.

5. Edith Cummings, the golf champion on whom Fitzgerald partly based the character of Jordan Baker. Fitzgerald knew Cummings through Ginevra King, his first serious love; King and Cummings were classmates at Westover, a girls' preparatory school in Connecticut. Cummings is shown here after winning the 1923 U.S. Women's Amateur tournament. Photo courtesy United States Golf Association.

APPENDIX 1
PERKINS' LETTERS OF CRITICISM

Below are printed the two letters from Perkins to Fitzgerald that record the editor's initial reactions to the novel. Readers should remember that Perkins is assessing the text of *Trimalchio*, not *The Great Gatsby*. For the larger correspondence surrounding the composition of the novel, see *Dear Scott/Dear Max*, pp. 60–94. The originals of Fitzgerald's letters, and carbon copies of Perkins' letters (from which the texts below are taken), are in the Scribners archives at Princeton University Library. Perkins' handwritten cancellations and additions to the ribbon copies were transferred to the carbons by his secretary; the final readings are given here.

Nov. 18, 1924

Dear Scott:

I think the novel is a wonder. I'm taking it home to read again and shall then write my impressions in full;—but it has vitality to an extraordinary degree, and glamour, and a great deal of underlying thought of unusual quality. It has a kind of mystic atmosphere at times that you infused into parts of "Paradise" and have not since used. It is a marvelous fusion, into a unity of presentation, of the extraordinary incongruities of life today. And as for sheer writing, it's astonishing.

Now deal with this question: various gentlemen here don't like the title,—in fact none like it but me. To me, the strange incongruity of the words in it sound the note of the book. But the objectors are more practical men than I. Consider as quickly as you can the question of a change.

But if you do not change, you will have to leave that note off the wrap.[1] Its presence would injure it too much;—and good as the

---

[1] Fitzgerald had evidently written a note for the dust jacket, perhaps identifying Trimalchio as a character in the *Satyricon*. The note does not survive in the Scribners files at Princeton.

wrap always seemed, it now seems a masterpiece for this book. So judge of the value of the title when it stands alone and write or cable your decision the instant you can.

With congratulations, I am,

Yours,

[Maxwell E. Perkins]

November 20, 1924

Dear Scott:

I think you have every kind of right to be proud of this book. It is an extraordinary book, suggestive of all sorts of thoughts and moods. You adopted exactly the right method of telling it, that of employing a narrator who is more of a spectator than an actor: this puts the reader upon a point of observation on a higher level than that on which the characters stand and at a distance that gives perspective. In no other way could your irony have been so immensely effective, nor the reader have been enabled so strongly to feel at times the strangeness of human circumstance in a vast heedless universe. In the eyes of Dr. Eckleberg various readers will see different significances; but their presence gives a superb touch to the whole thing: great unblinking eyes, expressionless, looking down upon the human scene. It's magnificent!

I could go on praising the book and speculating on its various elements, and meanings, but points of criticism are more important now. I think you are right in feeling a certain slight sagging in chapters six and seven, and I don't know how to suggest a remedy. I hardly doubt that you will find one and I am only writing to say that I think it does need something to hold up here to the pace set and ensuing. I have only two actual criticisms:—

One is that among a set of characters marvelously palpable and vital—I would know Tom Buchanan if I met him on the street and would avoid him—Gatsby is somewhat vague. The reader's eyes can never quite focus upon him, his outlines are dim. Now everything about Gatsby is more or less a mystery i.e. more or less vague, and this may be somewhat of an artistic intention, but I think it is mistaken. Couldn't <u>he</u> be physically described as distinctly as the others, and couldn't you add one or two characteristics like the use of that phrase "old sport",—not verbal, but physical ones, perhaps. I think that for some reason or other a reader—this was true of Mr. Scribner and of Louise[2]—gets an idea that Gatsby is a much older man than he is, although you have the writer say that he is little older than himself. But this would be avoided if on his first appearance he was seen as vividly as Daisy and Tom are, for instance;—and I do not think your scheme would be impaired if you made him so.

The other point is also about Gatsby: his career must remain mysterious, of course. But in the end you make it pretty clear that his wealth came through his connection with Wolfsheim. You also suggest this much earlier. Now almost all readers numerically are going to be puzzled by his having all this wealth and are going to feel entitled to an explanation. To give a distinct and definite one would be, of course, utterly absurd. It did occur to me though, that you might here and there interpolate some phrases, and possibly incidents, little touches of various kinds, that would suggest that he was in some active way mysteriously engaged. You do have him called on the telephone, but couldn't he be seen once or twice consulting at his parties with people of some sort of mysterious significance, from the political, the gambling, the sporting world, or whatever it may be. I know I am floundering, but that fact may help you to see what I mean. The <u>total</u> lack of an explanation through so large a part of the story does seem to me a defect;—or not of an explanation, but of the suggestion of an explanation. I wish you were here so I could talk about it to you for then I know I could at least make you understand what I mean. What Gatsby did ought never to be definitely imparted, even if it could be. Whether he was an innocent tool in the hands of somebody else, or to what degree he was this, ought not to be explained. But if some sort of business activity of his were simply adumbrated, it would lend further probability to that part of the story.

There is one other point: in giving deliberately Gatsby's bio-

2 Charles Scribner, head of the firm, and Louise Saunders Perkins, the editor's wife.

graphy when he gives it to the narrator you do depart from the method of the narrative in some degree, for otherwise almost everything is told, and beautifully told, in the regular flow of it,— in the succession of events or in accompaniment with them. But you can't avoid the biography altogether. I thought you might find ways to let the truth of some of his claims like "Oxford" and his army career come out bit by bit in the course of actual narrative. I mention the point anyway for consideration in this interval before I send the proofs.

The general brilliant quality of the book makes me ashamed to make even these criticisms. The amount of meaning you get into a sentence, the dimensions and intensity of the impression you make a paragraph carry, are most extraordinary. The manuscript is full of phrases which make a scene blaze with life. If one enjoyed a rapid railroad journey I would compare the number and vividness of pictures your living words suggest, to the living scenes disclosed in that way. It seems in reading a much shorter book than it is, but it carries the mind through a series of experiences that one would think would require a book of three times its length.

The presentation of Tom, his place, Daisy and Jordan, and the unfolding of their characters is unequalled so far as I know. The description of the valley of ashes adjacent to the lovely country, the conversation and the action in Myrtle's apartment, the marvelous catalogue of those who came to Gatsby's house,—these are such things as make a man famous. And all these things, the whole pathetic episode, you have given a place in time and space, for with the help of T. J. Eckleberg and by an occasional glance at the sky, or the sea, or the city, you have imparted a sort of sense of eternity. You once told me you were not a <u>natural</u> writer—my God! You have plainly mastered the craft, of course; but you needed far more than craftsmanship for this.

> As ever,
> [Maxwell E. Perkins}

P.S. Why do you ask for a lower royalty on this than you had on the last book where it changed from 15% to 17½% after 20,000 and to 20% after 40,000? Did you do it in order to give us a better margin for advertising? We shall advertise very energetically anyhow and if you stick to the old terms you will sooner overcome the advance. Naturally we should like the ones you suggest better, but there is no reason you should get less on this than you did on the other.[3]

---

[3] In his 27 October 1924 letter to Perkins, Fitzgerald had asked for lower than normal escalating royalties: 15% to 50,000 copies and 20% thereafter. He answered this postscript from Perkins as follows in a letter written *c.* 1 December 1924: "I made the royalty smaller because I wanted to make up for all the money you've advanced these two years by letting it pay a sort of interest on it. But I see by calculating I made it too small – a difference of 2000 dollars. Let us call it 15% up to 40,000 and 20% after that. That's a good fair contract all around." These were in fact the final figures in Fitzgerald's contract with Scribners.

APPENDIX 2
NOTE ON TRIMALCHIO

Trimalchio, a freed slave who has grown wealthy, hosts a lavish banquet in one of the best-known chapters of the *Satyricon* by Petronius (*c.* AD 27–66). In translations, the chapter is usually entitled "The Party at Trimalchio's" or "Trimalchio's Feast"; it is one of the best accounts of domestic revelry to survive from the reign of the emperor Nero. The chapter is narrated by Encolpius, an observer and recorder rather than a participant.

Banquet scenes were conventions of classical literature (e.g., the *Symposia* of Plato and Xenophon). They were occasions for mild jesting and for conversations about art, literature, and philosophy. Trimalchio's party is a parody of this convention: most of the guests are inebriated and are disdainful of learning; their crude talk, in colloquial Latin, is largely about money and possessions.

Trimalchio himself is old and unattractive, bibulous and libidinous. His house, though, is spacious; his dining-room contains an impressively large water-clock; his servants are dressed in elaborate costumes. The banquet he hosts is ostentatious, with entertainments carefully rehearsed and staged. There are numerous courses of food and drink and several rounds of gifts for the guests, many of whom do not know Trimalchio and speak slightingly of him when he leaves the room.

The banquet becomes progressively more vinous; it ends with a drunken Trimalchio feigning death atop a mound of pillows, his hired trumpeters blaring a funeral march. The noise brings the city's fire crew; they kick in the door and cause chaos with water and axes. Encolpius and his friends escape into the night without bidding farewell to their host.

APPENDIX 3
NOTE ON EYESKIP

One of the most famous paragraphs in the novel occurs in Chapter I, in the account of Nick's first visit to the Buchanans' house. In holograph, the paragraph reads as follows:

> The only completely stationary object in the room seemed to be an enormous couch on which two young women were buoyed up as though upon an anchored balloon. They were both in white and their dresses were rippling and fluttering as if they had just been blown back in after a short flight around the house. I must have stood for a few moments on the threshold, dazzled by the alabaster light, listening to the whip and snap of the curtains and the groan of a picture on the wall. Then there was a boom as Tom Buchanan shut the rear windows and the caught wind died out about the room and the curtains and the rugs and the two young women ballooned slowly to the floor.[1]

Between holograph and galleys, the reading "on the threshold, dazzled by the alabaster light," disappears from the third sentence and, consequently, is missing from the first edition. This reading, in the handwritten draft, occupies one complete line – the fourth line on leaf 12, Chapter I. The positioning of the line on the leaf (see Illustration 2) arouses a suspicion that the typist's eye skipped from "moments" at the end of line 3 to "listening" at the beginning of line 5. Such eyeskip errors are common in typed transcriptions.[2]

The typescript made from this draft does not survive. One can therefore only speculate about what happened to the missing words. It is possible that the typist did copy "on the threshold, dazzled by the alabaster light," and that Fitzgerald struck out the words in revising. It is also possible that the typist skipped the words and that Fitzgerald did not notice the mistake, since no error in grammar or logic would have been introduced.

On the basis only of these speculations, one cannot restore "on the

---

[1] Three corrections have been made in the holograph text for this rendering: "a enormous" to "an enormous"; "apon" to "upon"; and "woman ballooned" to "women ballooned".

[2] Fitzgerald always used copyists; he did not type.

threshold, dazzled by the alabaster light," to the text of *Trimalchio*. Readers, however, should know the history of the sentence and should test both versions against their own sense of Fitzgerald's style. The passage occurs on p. 10 of this edition of *Trimalchio*.

Made in the USA
Middletown, DE
07 April 2017